100 BASEBALL LEGENDS

WHO SHAPED SPORTS HISTORY

RUSSELL ROBERTS

sourcebooks
eXplore

Copyright © 2003, 2023 by Sourcebooks
Text by Russell Roberts
Cover design by Will Riley
Internal illustrations by AAARep/Ricardo Galvão
Cover and internal design © 2023 by Sourcebooks

Published by Sourcebooks eXplore, an imprint of Sourcebooks Kids
P.O. Box 4410, Naperville, Illinois 60567-4410
(630) 961-3900
sourcebookskids.com

Originally published in 2003 by Bluewood Books, an imprint of The Siyeh Group, Inc.

Library of Congress Cataloging-in-Publication Data is on file with the Library of Congress.

Source of Production: Versa Press, East Peoria, Illinois, USA
Date of Production: July 2023
Run Number: 5030857

Printed and bound in the United States of America.
VP 10 9 8 7 6 5 4 3 2 1

CONTENTS

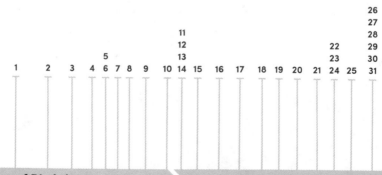

Timeline of Birthdates

1855 — 1903

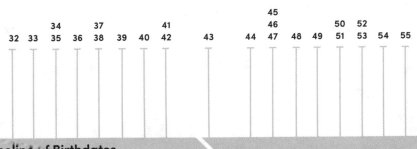

Timeline of Birthdates

1904

1925

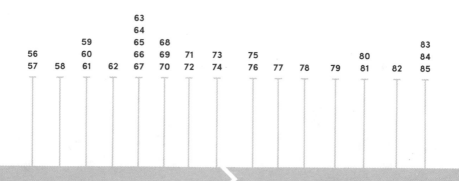

1926

1946

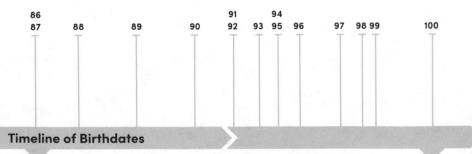

Timeline of Birthdates

1947   1974

INTRODUCTION

THIS IS a book about one hundred of the greatest baseball players to ever play the game. Such a list is highly subjective; choosing a group of the best players from more than 125 years of major league baseball is extremely difficult.

Some choices, of course, come easily. Certain players belong on any list of greats, be it one hundred or twenty. Big names such as Babe Ruth, Lou Gehrig, Cy Young, Ty Cobb, Christy Mathewson, Walter Johnson, Joe DiMaggio, Ted Williams, Willie Mays, Mickey Mantle, and Hank Aaron fall into that category.

Then there are those who are right below them—those whose pitching or hitting feats just miss being grouped with the immortals. These include players like Tris Speaker, Charlie Gehringer, Mel Ott, Yogi Berra, Jackie Robinson, Bob Gibson, Sandy Koufax, and Reggie Jackson. Most ardent baseball fans would agree that these names also deserve to be included on any list of the sport's legends.

However, once you get beyond the top twenty to thirty immortals, and the next twenty-five to thirty who fall just beneath them, deciding who should fill out the rest of the one hundred is less obvious. You could base selections on pure statistics, but numbers often do not tell the whole story.

Take Pee Wee Reese, for example. He did not have great career statistics, yet for years he was the heart and soul of the Brooklyn Dodgers in the 1940s and 1950s. The intangible benefits that he brought to the team were invaluable and helped them win. Reese is only one of many players whose careers amounted to much more than great statistics—and who were deservedly inducted into the Baseball Hall of Fame.

It's clear that evaluating players mainly by statistics can cause strong debate because many players had careers with very similar accomplishments. Was Al Kaline a better hitter than Goose Goslin? Both men had similar offensive numbers in careers that lasted nearly twenty years. But Kaline played into the 1970s, while Goslin's career ended in 1937. Who was more valuable to the success of the Big Red Machine—Joe Morgan or Tony Perez? Statistics will not help you decide here either because these players were very close statistically. And besides, the relative impact of any statistic can be debated: Were Morgan's stolen bases as important as Perez's home runs?

This type of debate is what makes baseball the fascinating sport that it is and helps fuel perpetual interest in the game. Unique among all sports, baseball cannot be understood through statistics alone, although numbers do provide a broad yardstick by which players can be evaluated.

For as long as baseball has been played—and will be played—the debate rages on as to who were the greatest players in history. As you read through this book, you may find yourself in agreement with every player selected, or you may shake your head and exclaim, "How could they write a book about baseball legends and leave out _____?" Either way, we hope that you thoroughly enjoy the biographies presented here. Perhaps you will admit that, while your favorite player might not have made our list, the one hundred included here did indeed leave a lasting impact on the great game of baseball.

CONNIE MACK was involved in major league baseball as a player, a manager, and an owner for more than sixty years, which is much longer than anyone else in the sport's history.

He was born Cornelius McGillicuddy, but Mack said that his family always used the shortened form of his name. In Massachusetts, Mack worked in factories during his youth. Yet whenever he got leisure time, he played baseball. When he lost his job in a shoe factory, he decided to make his living in baseball.

After playing pro ball for several years as a good-field, no-hit catcher, Mack became the player-manager of the Pittsburgh Pirates in 1894 but was fired at the end of the 1896 season. He then accepted an offer from his good friend Ban Johnson, president of the Western League, to pilot a team in Milwaukee. In 1901, Johnson reorganized the Western League into a viable competitor for the National League—the only major

league in existence at the time—and called it the American League. Subsequently, Mack was assigned to manage the Philadelphia Athletics and became part owner of the franchise.

Mack won the pennant with the A's in 1902 and 1905. Then from 1910 to 1914, the A's dominated the league with the team's first dynasty. They won four pennants and three World Series during those years. Mack built his team around his "$100,000 infield," including third baseman Frank "Home Run" Baker and second baseman Eddie Collins, as well as star pitchers Charles "Chief" Bender and Eddie Plank.

However, after losing the World Series in 1914, Mack began selling off his star players because he was fearful that he might have to match the salaries that the new rival Federal League was offering. Stripped of their talent, the A's plunged to the basement.

By the late 1920s, Mack had built another dynasty. In 1929, the A's won the first of three straight pennants, with players such as slugger Jimmie Foxx and fireball pitcher Lefty Grove. The team won two more world championships but lost the 1931 World Series. By then, America was mired in the Great Depression, and money woes were again haunting Mack. Once more, he sold off his stars' contracts, and the A's sank to the second division, where they remained for most of the rest of his managerial tenure.

Soft-spoken and courteous, Mack directed his team like a gentleman. He rarely argued with umpires, and he managed from the dugout dressed in a business suit and a tie instead of a uniform.

In 1940, Mack became majority owner of the team. He retired as manager of the A's in 1950. After he sold the franchise in 1954, the new owner moved the team to Kansas City.

During the third game of the 1903 World Series between Boston Americans of the American League and Pittsburgh Pirates of the National League—the first World Series ever played—Boston pitcher **CY YOUNG** was sitting in street clothes in the team offices counting receipts. Suddenly Young received a frantic call: put your uniform on, warm up, and go into the game in relief.

Young did, even though he had pitched the first game of the Series two days before. Later he appeared in two more games and won them both as Boston upset Pittsburgh.

The pitcher was rubber-armed Denton True Young, who won more games than anyone else in baseball history over his twenty-two-year career. His unusual nickname resulted from the damage he supposedly once inflicted on a wooden fence while warming up. Someone said it looked as if a cyclone had hit the fence, and soon people were calling him "Cy" for short.

Born in 1867 in Gilmore, Ohio, Young was dismissed as "just another big farmer" by major league baseball who's who, including the legendary Cap Anson. However, after signing with the Canton team of the Tri-State League in 1890, Young's contract was sold to the Cleveland Spiders of the National League. On August 6, Young achieved his first major league victory and beat Anson's team, 8–1. After that, Anson attempted to buy Young's contract for $1,000. "I might make a pitcher out of him in a few years," Anson said.

Cleveland rejected the offer, and as it turned out, Young didn't need help from Anson—or anyone else—to become a pitcher.

After winning nine games for the Spiders that year, Young notched 27 victories in 1891, and then compiled a sparkling 36–12 record in 1892 with a 1.93 earned run average (ERA). Thereafter, he was one of the top pitchers during the 1890s, piling up yearly victory totals of 34, 26, 35, and 28. Along the way, he developed a reputation for stamina and control unsurpassed by any other pitcher.

In 1901, Young jumped to the Boston club of the newly formed American League. Considered washed up at the age of thirty-four, Young defied the doubters by winning 33, 32, 28, and 26 games in his first four seasons with Boston. In 1904, he pitched a perfect game against the Philadelphia Athletics.

Finally, in 1911, time caught up to the forty-four-year-old Young. After a 7–9 season, he retired. Young pitched more than 900 games and 7,000 innings in his major league career, and his lifetime victory total of 511 will almost certainly never be broken.

Young was elected to the Hall of Fame in 1937. The Cy Young Award for pitching excellence is named after him.

JOE "IRON MAN" MCGINNITY's career wasn't long—only ten years—but in that short time span, he managed to win 247 games.

Born in Rock Island, Illinois, McGinnity initially seemed destined for nothing but obscurity after spending two mediocre seasons in the minor leagues in the early 1890s. Discouraged and dogged by health concerns, McGinnity quit professional baseball and opened a saloon. But then, two things happened. First, McGinnity regained his health. Then he developed a devastating pitch he called "Old Sal"—a slow sidearm curve ball that proved nearly impossible to hit.

With his baseball career revitalized, McGinnity won 10 games in 1898 for the Peoria Distillers minor league team. That season won him a contract with the Baltimore Orioles of the National League in 1899, where he won a league leading 28 games.

McGinnity spent the next few years bouncing between a couple of different teams. However, in 1902, McGinnity joined the New York Giants of the National League. The Giants were to be McGinnity's final stop, and the team with which he would pitch his way into the Hall of Fame.

The pitcher made an immediate impact on the club the following year. He won a league-leading 31 games and notched 44 complete games—a twentieth-century National League record. The following year, he won 35 games to again lead the league, with 38 complete games. Ironically, his Iron Man nickname doesn't stem from hurling so many complete games, but rather from a stint as an ironworker earlier in his life.

In 1904, McGinnity and Christy Mathewson combined to win 68 games—another twentieth-century National League record for two pitchers on the same team.

The following year, McGinnity "slipped" to 21 victories. However, together with Mathewson on the mound, the Giants roared to the pennant. In the 1905 World Series, the Giants shut out the Philadelphia A's four times, with Mathewson throwing three whitewashes. McGinnity threw the fourth shutout.

In 1906, McGinnity again led the league with 27 victories, but it was his last very good year. After two subsequent so-so seasons, he was released at his own request so that he could manage in the minor leagues. He continued to pitch during his managing career, though, and in 1925, he had a 6–6 record for a team in Dubuque, of which he was manager and part owner. At the time, he was fifty-four years old and a true "iron man" of the mound.

He was elected to the Hall of Fame in 1946.

JOHN JOSEPH MCGRAW was that rarest of commodities because he was a good ballplayer and a great manager. In either capacity, he was argumentative, hard-nosed, and hot-tempered—always ready to fight and possessed with an overwhelming desire to win. During his tenure as the New York Giants manager in the early part of the twentieth century, he was as dominant a figure sitting in the dugout as any player on the field.

Born in Truxton, New York, and the oldest of eight children, McGraw watched helplessly when diphtheria killed his mother and four of his siblings when he was eleven years old. To escape the beatings of his grieving father, he ran away from home at the age of twelve.

When he was only eighteen, McGraw joined the Baltimore Orioles in the American Association and went along when the team entered the National League in 1892. He was the third baseman on one of the rowdiest teams in baseball history, a team that believed spiking both opponents and umpires was acceptable if it resulted in a victory. One of McGraw's favorite tricks was to grab an opponent's belt to slow him down and stop him from scoring.

McGraw's best season with the Orioles was in 1898, when he hit .342 and led the league with 143 runs scored. However, it was when he became manager of the National League's New York Giants in 1902 at the age of twenty-nine that McGraw found immortality.

Over the next thirty years, McGraw cajoled, browbeat, and bullied his players to three World Series titles and ten pennants. McGraw built three powerhouse teams during his time as Giants manager. The Giants won the pennant in 1904 and 1905, won three straight pennants from 1911 to 1913, and won four straight again from 1921 to 1924. Their world championships came in 1905, 1921, and 1922.

McGraw was a master of hit-and-run play of the dead-ball era. Hit-and-run play was when a base hit, a stolen base, and a walk constituted an offensive explosion. McGraw was as confrontational managing as he had been playing, always yelling and screaming at his players to get them to do his bidding. Some players didn't take kindly to his tongue-lashings. After one verbal confrontation with first baseman Bill Terry, the two did not speak for two years. However, McGraw was also known to be very patient with young players and could be generous off the field. He often gave money to former players who had financial problems.

McGraw retired in the middle of the 1932 season for health reasons. During his thirty-one-year career as the Giants manager, his teams had only three losing seasons.

Considered by many to be the best shortstop in major league history, **JOHANNES PETER "HONUS" WAGNER** was also one of baseball's greatest offensive threats as a hitter and a base runner.

Wagner was born in 1874 in Mansfield, Pennsylvania. As a teenager, he apprenticed in his brother's barbershop but tended to neglect his duties for baseball. One story has it that Wagner once even left a man half-shaven and asleep in a chair while he went off to play a game. That night, his brother is said to have fired him.

Wagner was then able to devote plenty of time to baseball. After a minor league stint, he joined the Louisville Colonels of the National League in 1897. He quickly became the team's star, posting batting averages of .338, .299, and .336 over his first three seasons. Unfortunately, the franchise folded after the 1899 season. However, the Louisville owner was Barney Dreyfuss, who also owned the Pittsburgh Pirates. Dreyfuss transferred Wagner's contract to Pittsburgh.

Wagner rewarded Dreyfuss's faith in him by leading the National League in hitting in 1900 with a .381 average, as well as leads in doubles, triples, and slugging averages. He would go on to win seven more batting titles and five more slugging crowns. He also led the league several times in doubles, triples, and runs batted in.

Wagner was a barrel-chested man with shoulders that were said to be broad enough to serve dinner on. Nevertheless, he was an extremely fast runner, leading the league in steals five times and earning the nickname "The Flying Dutchman." His highest base stealing total was 61 in 1907. Overall, he stole 722 bases during his career.

Despite his speed, Wagner was anything but graceful on the playing field. One newspaper claimed that, when he ran, the bowlegged Wagner looked like a propeller. However, he was a sure-handed fielder, who rarely missed a grounder at shortstop. He supposedly dug balls out of the dirt with his huge hands and threw them so hard to first that any pebbles he scooped up traveled along with the ball.

Wagner appeared in two World Series, in 1903 and 1909. In the second fall classic, he hit .333, outshining the great Ty Cobb in their only face-to-face meeting. Wagner retired after the 1917 season and finished his career with a .327 lifetime batting average and 3,418 hits. In 1936, he was one of the first five players named to the Hall of Fame.

Decades after he last played, Wagner gained new popularity in the 1980s when his 1910 cigarette baseball card sold for more than $450,000. One rumor propagated that it was valuable because the ballplayer did not approve of tobacco and stopped production of the card. However, the story is false. It is simply an old card of a great ballplayer.

NAPOLEON "LARRY" LAJOIE was such a popular player in baseball's early years that when he played for the Cleveland Blues, they even changed the team name to the "Naps" in his honor.

Born in Woonsocket, Rhode Island, Lajoie played only a few months of minor league ball before he joined the Philadelphia Phillies in 1896. For the next five seasons, Lajoie was a star with the Phillies—he never hit lower than .324, and in 1898, he led the league with 43 doubles and 127 RBIs. The Phillies seemed ready to shed their also-ran status and become pennant contenders in the National League.

However, around that time, Lajoie and the Phillies were embroiled in a salary dispute. In 1901, the disgusted Lajoie jumped to the Philadelphia A's of the new rival American League, who offered him $6,000 annually on a four-year contract.

Lajoie hit .422 in 1901 for the A's—the highest American League batting average in the twentieth century. He also smashed 14 homers and drove in 125 runs to win the league's Triple Crown. However, the Phillies were not done, and they got a court injunction that forbade Lajoie from playing for any other team in Philadelphia except the Phillies. The injunction was only valid in the state of Pennsylvania, so the A's promptly traded Lajoie to the Cleveland Blues (who later became the Cleveland Indians and are now the Cleveland Guardians).

With the Blues, Lajoie kept up his hitting rampage, batting .355 and .381 in 1903 and 1904 to win two more batting titles. Over the next ten years, he continued to star for Cleveland, hitting over .300 seven times. Lajoie became Cleveland's player-manager in 1905 and lasted until late in the 1909 season, when he quit as manager because he felt the pressure was affecting his play. In

1910, Lajoie was locked in a fierce battle with Ty Cobb for the batting crown. The prize for winning the title was a new car. His rival was so disliked throughout baseball that, in the last game of the season, the St. Louis Browns manager ordered his third baseman to play deep, allowing Lajoie to get six bunt singles and win the title. However, the ploy was exposed, and while Cobb and Lajoie both won cars, Cobb has gone down as the official batting champion by one point, .385 to .384.

After three more great years with Cleveland, Lajoie began to slip in 1914, when he hit only .258. He spent the next two years back with the A's, and then retired after the 1916 season. Lajoie finished his career with a .338 lifetime batting average, 3,242 hits, and 1,599 RBIs. He was elected to the Hall of Fame in 1937.

MIKE KELLY was the first superstar in baseball—a man who played the game hard and fell from the pinnacle of success just as hard.

Mike "King" Kelly was born in 1857 in Troy, New York. He was playing for the Cincinnati Reds in the late 1870s when they neglected to protect him, and Adrian Constantine "Cap" Anson's Chicago White Stockings snapped him up.

While with Chicago, Kelly blossomed into a star. He led the National League in hitting twice, with a .354 average in 1884 and .388 in 1886. Mostly a right fielder and a catcher, he played every other position except pitcher and played each with great skill. It was with Chicago that Kelly got his nickname of "King." Fans began calling him that because of his off-the-field clothing—a London silk hat, a jeweled scarf, and patent leather shoes.

However, it was for stealing bases that Kelly was best known. He stole 84 in 1887; the first-year totals were kept for steals, followed by years of 56, 68, and 51.

Kelly had an unmatched flair for stealing bases that became so popular with the fans that they screamed out "Slide, Kelly, Slide!" whenever he got on, which inspired the song of the same name. Supposedly the inventor of the hook slide, Kelly's sliding technique, was described by one contemporary: "He would jump into the air ten feet from the sack, dive directly for it, dig one of his spiked shoes into the bag, and then swerve clear over on his side. Few second basemen had the nerve to block his hurricane dives."

Thanks to his hitting and base-running heroics, Kelly helped Chicago rule the National League during his tenure. However, with his black hair, good looks, and handlebar mustache, Kelly was also fond of drinking, and that ultimately led to a falling out with the puritanical Anson.

Eventually, Anson grew weary of Kelly's antics, and in 1887, he sold Kelly's contract to the Boston Beaneaters for $10,000, which was an unheard of sum for a ballplayer at that time. It was a total that got Kelly nicknamed "the $10,000 beauty." Welcoming Boston fans presented him with a house and a carriage drawn by two white horses. Kelly helped Boston win two pennants in three years, hitting .322, .318, and .294, but by 1890, his drinking caused him to gain weight and have trouble in the field. He hit only .189 in 1892.

After leaving baseball, Kelly tried to make a living on stage, but he caught pneumonia in late 1894. When Kelly slipped from the stretcher that was bringing him to the hospital, he proved one last time that he had not lost his flair, supposedly gasping, "This is my last slide." He died on November 8.

◆ **ANDREW "RUBE" FOSTER** was one of the pillars of early Black baseball—as a player, a manager, and a league organizer.

Born in Calvert, Texas, Foster dreamed as a boy of playing baseball despite his parents' wishes against it. When he was old enough, he left home to find diamond glory, but organized baseball was closed to Black athletes. Foster was forced to pursue his dream in other ways, bouncing around the semi-pro leagues for a few years.

At six foot four and 225 pounds, Foster was a big man with a blazing fastball and a nasty screwball that he threw from a submarine delivery. After perfecting his pitching style, he joined the Philadelphia Cuban X-Giants in 1903, one of the all-Black teams that played close to major league caliber. That year he beat the Philadelphia Giants four times in a seven-game series to win the Black world championships for his team. The next year, he jumped to the Philly Giants and beat his old team twice in three games

for that year's championship, striking out 18 batters in one game.

Foster became such a dominating pitcher that, following one of his victories, one newspaper simply wrote the headline, "Foster Pitched, That's All." The tragedy is that early Black baseball records are so incomplete that it will never be known for certain how many games Foster won in his career.

However, as brilliant a pitcher as Foster was, he was equally adept at managing. He became player-manager of the Chicago American Giants in 1910 and instituted an aggressive, run-oriented game that drove opponents crazy. Some of his favorite tactics were the hit-and-run bunt and the triple steal. He also developed the steal-and-bunt, where a man on first would take off and the batter would bunt to third. If the third baseman threw to first, the runner continued to third. If he held the ball, then there would be runners on first and second.

Foster pitched for Chicago until 1915 and managed the team until 1920. That year, he organized the Negro National League in an attempt "to do something for the race" and put Black baseball on a par with the white league. He served as league president and secretary for six years. Foster struggled desperately to keep the league afloat, moving players from team to team to strike a competitive balance and working long hours on administrative matters.

In 1926, Foster snapped under the strain, suffering a mental breakdown that had him hospitalized. He never recovered and died in 1930. Rube Foster was elected to the Hall of Fame in 1981.

One of baseball's all-time greatest pitchers, **CHRISTY MATHEWSON**, was an educated and clean cut all-American boy in an era when the game was filled with tough, hard-drinking competitors.

Born in Factoryville, Pennsylvania, Mathewson attended Bucknell University, where he starred in baseball, basketball, and football. He was also class president and a member of the literary society. In 1899, Mathewson left college to play professional baseball. He signed with the National League's New York Giants, and in 1901, his first full year in the majors, he won 20 games.

After a mediocre season in 1902, Mathewson then reeled off a string of three consecutive seasons, in which he won 30 games or more and led the league in strikeouts each year. In 1905, he led the league in victories with 31, as well as in earned run average (ERA), with 1.27. In the World Series that year against the Philadelphia Athletics, all of Mathewson's sensational pitching skills were on display. He shut out the A's three times in six days, allowing them just 14 hits over that span as the Giants took the Series in five games.

For the next nine seasons, Mathewson won at least 22 games a year. During that time, he led the league in victories three times—including a career high 37 wins in 1908—had the league's lowest ERA four times and was the strikeout leader twice. He would go on to win 373 games over his illustrious career, including 80 lifetime shutouts.

"He could throw a ball into a tin cup at pitching range," one player remembered, but pinpoint control was only one of Mathewson's talents. Among his repertoire of pitches was one he developed called the fadeaway, which is similar to a modern screwball.

Mathewson was not a humble man, though, and sometimes his holier-than-thou attitude rubbed players the wrong way.

However, despite their vastly different natures, Mathewson was the favorite player of crusty Giants' manager John McGraw (see no. 4), who treated him like a son. In 1916, Mathewson, his long pitching career virtually at an end, was traded to the Cincinnati Reds to be their manager. Two years later, at age thirty-eight, Mathewson enlisted in the U.S. Army, which was involved in World War I. Sent overseas, he was the victim of a poison gas attack. He never recovered from the effects of the gas and developed tuberculosis. He died in a sanitarium in New York on October 7, 1925.

At his funeral, John McGraw cried bitterly at the loss of his beloved "Matty" at such a young age. Mathewson was one of the first five players voted to baseball's Hall of Fame in 1936.

A fierce and sometimes crazed competitor, **TY COBB** was described by many who played against him and saw him play as the most feared and disliked baseball player in history. Yet those very same people conceded that he was perhaps also the greatest all-around player the game has ever seen.

Born Tyrus Raymond Cobb in 1886 in Narrows, Georgia, Cobb was ticketed for a career in medicine or law by his father, but he wanted to try baseball instead. In early August 1905, he was leading the South Atlantic League (also known as the Sally League) in hitting when he got word that his father had been shot to death by his mother, who allegedly mistook him for an intruder. Many speculated that Cobb competed so ferociously throughout his career to justify his late father's faith in him.

Soon after the incident, Cobb's contract was sold to the Detroit Tigers. He arrived as a scared and young rookie. His combative personality made him react poorly to the

severe hazing that rookies received, such as when his teammates cut his bats in half. As a result, he developed a "Cobb-against-the-world" attitude that characterized his entire career.

On the field, Cobb was a demon of a player. He piled up 892 lifetime stolen bases—a record that stood until it was broken by Lou Brock in 1977—tallying 96 in 1915, another record that stood for almost fifty years. Cobb's record of stealing home fifty times over his career will almost certainly remain unbroken.

Just as important as speed to Cobb was how he stole those bases. True to his fiery personality, he never just slid into a base but launched himself like a missile. Adding to the anxiety of infielders was a persistent rumor that he also sharpened his spikes.

Cobb was sensational at bat. Beginning in 1906, he hit .300 or better for the next 23 consecutive seasons—the remainder of his career. He won the league batting title a record twelve times, nine of which were consecutive. He also hit better than .400 twice: .420 in 1911 and .410 in 1912. His finished his career with a lifetime batting average of .366, which is another almost certainly untouchable record, and 4,191 lifetime hits as the second on the all-time list to date.

Cobb played for the Tigers for twenty-two years and helped lead the team to three straight pennants from 1907 through to 1909. Unfortunately, they still lost the World Series each year. He was Detroit's player-manager from 1921 to 1926 before being released.

After two seasons with the Philadelphia A's, Cobb retired in 1929. He was among the first group of five players elected to the Hall of Fame in 1936.

Despite numerous personal and health problems that plagued his career, **GROVER CLEVELAND ALEXANDER** ranks among the top three or four pitchers who ever played baseball.

Alexander was born in Elba, Nebraska, one of thirteen children. Growing up, he perfected his pitching accuracy by hurling rocks at chickens and turkeys to kill them for dinner.

Playing semipro ball, Alexander was knocked unconscious when he was struck between the eyes by a throw. From then on, he was plagued with epileptic seizures for the rest of his life.

Alexander began his major league career with the National League's Philadelphia Phillies in 1911, winning 28 games in a spectacular rookie season. After winning 19 and 22 games over the next two years, Alexander put together four of the most brilliant consecutive seasons any pitcher ever had. From 1914 to 1917, he led the league each year with

27, 31, 33, and 30 victories. He also led the league each year in complete games and strikeouts, and in shutouts and earned run average (ERA) three times.

After the 1917 season, the Phillies traded Alexander to the Chicago Cubs after a salary dispute. He was drafted in 1918 and deployed to France to fight in World War I. He suffered hearing loss in one ear as a result of a shelling, and when he returned from the war, he began drinking heavily.

Alexander pitched for the Cubs for several seasons and was a two-time, 20-game winner. However, his reputation as a drinker and difficult personality caused the Cubs to waive him to the St. Louis Cardinals in the middle of the 1926 season. Then, to the surprise of many, he won nine games for the Cardinals and helped them capture the pennant.

After this, the thirty-nine-year-old Alexander achieved his greatest success in the World Series against the Babe Ruth–led New York Yankees. After pitching two complete game victories in games one and six, he didn't expect to pitch again. But when the Yankees loaded the bases in the seventh inning of the seventh game, manager Rogers Hornsby called on Alexander in relief to pitch to New York's slugger, Tony Lazzeri. Although he was feeling hungover from drinking the night before, Alexander fanned Lazzeri on four pitches. He threw two more scoreless innings to preserve the victory that earned the Cardinals the world title.

That was Alexander's final moment of glory. He retired in 1930 and struggled with epilepsy and alcoholism for the remainder of his life. His 373 lifetime victories—tying him with Christy Mathewson—trail only Cy Young and Walter Johnson among all pitchers. He was elected to the Hall of Fame in 1938.

◆ **JOE MCCARTHY** has both the highest career and World Series winning percentage of any manager in baseball history.

Born in Philadelphia, Pennsylvania, McCarthy never played a game in the big leagues. He had fifteen seasons in the minors, and several of those were spent as a player-manager. In 1921, he quit playing but remained a manager, winning two pennants with the Louisville Colonels of the American Association. In 1926, the low-performing Chicago Cubs of the National League hired him as their manager.

A strict disciplinarian, McCarthy soon molded the Cubs into a competitive team. They improved steadily during his first three years, and in 1929, Chicago finally won its first pennant since 1918. However, they lost to the Philadelphia A's in the World Series in five games.

During the following season, McCarthy became dissatisfied because he felt Rogers Hornsby, the great second baseman to play for the Cubs in 1929, was undermining his authority. With the team in second place, McCarthy left with four games remaining in the season, and Hornsby replaced him as manager.

McCarthy was not unemployed for long when the New York Yankees recruited him after the 1930 season. Despite having talent like Babe Ruth and Lou Gehrig on the roster, the Yankees had gone two years without a pennant.

After finishing second in 1931, McCarthy's Yankees won both the pennant and the World Series in 1932, beating his old Chicago Cubs team. The Yankees finished second over the next three years. Then, in 1936, a rookie outfielder named Joe DiMaggio joined the team, and McCarthy's Yankees began an incredible success streak. From that year through 1943, the Yankees won seven American League pennants and six world championships—an unparalleled achievement at the time.

McCarthy was called a "push-button manager" by critics, who believed that all he had to do was select the right player in order to win because he had such a great team. However, McCarthy was a master strategist, and he knew how to get the most out each individual on a team. For example, when World War II stripped baseball of all their top starting pitchers, McCarthy was the first to get a significant contribution from his bullpen to pick up the slack.

In 1946, he left the Yankees for health reasons but returned to baseball in 1948 as manager of the Boston Red Sox. However, he lost the pennant to the Cleveland Indians in a playoff in 1948 and finished second in 1949 by one game to the Yankees. He retired during the next season. McCarthy was inducted into the Hall of Fame in 1957.

Did **"SHOELESS JOE" JACKSON** participate in the "Black Sox" Scandal to throw the 1919 World Series? Does he deserve to be in the Hall of Fame? These questions will forever swirl around the reputation of Jackson, one of the greatest hitters of all time.

Jackson was born in Pickens County, South Carolina, in 1889. As a youth, he worked a dozen hours a day in the cotton mills, from which his only escape was baseball. The most accepted version of how he received his nickname is that he played a game with new shoes, but then the next day, he played the game in his stocking feet because his feet hurt.

After playing briefly with the Philadelphia A's in 1908 and 1909, Jackson's contract was sold to the Cleveland Indians in 1910. In 1911, his first full season in the majors, Jackson exploded onto the baseball stage, hitting a blistering .408. He followed that up with averages of .395, .373, and .338.

Despite Jackson's hitting heroics, the Indians were a mediocre team that by 1914 had fallen into last place. Late in the 1915 season, Jackson was traded to the Chicago White Sox. The Sox were building a championship team, and Jackson became a major contributor. In 1916, he hit .341 and led the league in triples, racking up 21. In 1917, he batted .301 and helped lead Chicago to a world championship, where he hit .304 in the World Series victory over the New York Giants.

After wartime service in a shipyard limited Jackson's play to only 17 games in 1918, he came back and hit .351 the next year as the Sox again won the pennant. Though heavily favored in the World Series against the Cincinnati Reds, the Sox lost in eight games.

In 1920, Jackson hit .382, but after the season concluded, a grand jury investigated charges that eight Sox players—including Jackson—had accepted bribes to deliberately lose the 1919 Series. Supposedly, the eight "Black Sox" confessed, but their confessions were lost.

Jackson claimed that he took no part in the fix, and his performance in the Series seemed to belie his involvement. He had hit .375, had six RBIs, and played errorless in the field. However, he admitted that he received $5,000 as a reward after the Sox lost.

With little direct evidence of their guilt, the eight players were acquitted in court. But the newly named baseball "czar," Commissioner Kenesaw Mountain Landis, permanently barred the eight players from baseball after the 1920 season.

Jackson's lifetime batting average is .356—the third highest ever—but because of the scandal, he is not eligible to be included in the Hall of Fame.

Known as "The Big Train" because of the blinding speed of his fastball, **WALTER JOHNSON** tallied more than 400 lifetime victories despite pitching for one of the worst teams in the American League for his entire career.

Born in Humboldt, Kansas, Johnson was a nineteen-year-old pitcher terrorizing batters in the Idaho State League when the Washington Senators of the American League signed him on the recommendation of a traveling liquor salesman. Johnson had a lanky build, broad shoulders, and extremely long arms. He flung the ball toward the plate with a slingshot motion that froze opposing batters.

According to a famous legend about Johnson's terrific speed, a batter once left the batter's box after futilely swinging at Johnson's first two pitches. Informed by the umpire that he had one swing left, the frustrated hitter said, "I know. You can have the next one. It won't do me any good."

From 1907 through to 1927, Johnson pitched exclusively for the Senators, which at the time was frequently mediocre and occasionally horrible. "First in war, first in peace, and last in the American League," was a familiar refrain used to describe the team.

Despite that, Johnson won 416 games, standing second only to Cy Young's record of 511 lifetime victories. In 1910, Johnson won 25 games while striking out 313 men, and in 1912, he notched 32 victories while fanning 303 batters. Continuing on in 1913, he won the most games of his career, totaling 36. He won 20 or more games for ten straight seasons, led the league in strikeouts twelve times, and threw 110 shutouts—the highest total in baseball history. His strikeout record of 3,508 was the most by a pitcher until 1983.

As intimidating as he was on the mound, Johnson had a secret fear of hitting opposing batters. "I wouldn't think of hitting a man," he said. "I know I'm capable of killing him if I do."

The Senators finally put together a pennant-winning team, and in 1924, in the twilight of his fabulous career, Johnson finally made it to the World Series. He lost two games but was marvelous in relief in the Series finale and was the winning pitcher when the Senators pulled out an improbable victory over the New York Giants. Johnson pitched brilliantly during their two winning games in the 1925 Series against Pittsburgh, but fatigue got the better of him in the seventh and deciding game, and the Pirates rallied to win the Series.

Johnson managed the Cleveland Indians and the Senators following his retirement after the 1927 season. He was one of the first five players elected to the Hall of Fame in 1936.

A man known as "The Gray Eagle" for the way he swooped in from center field and caught fly balls, and if anyone is in the Hall of Fame for defense as much as offense, that person is **TRIS SPEAKER**.

Tristram Speaker was born in 1888 in Hubbard, Texas, and spent much of his youth riding horses and playing baseball. A natural right-hander, one day he fell off his horse and broke his right arm so severely that he had to learn how to throw and bat left-handed.

At age seventeen, Speaker signed his first professional baseball contract. After a short stint in the North Texas League, he joined the Boston Red Sox of the American League and batted .309 as a rookie in 1909. For the next nineteen seasons, he would fail to hit .300 only once.

Speaker's arrival boosted the Red Sox from mediocrity to pennant contenders. Boston won the World Series in 1912 and 1915 with major contributions from Speaker, who

hit .383 and .322 during the two seasons, respectively.

Despite Speaker's ability, it was his misfortune to play during the same era and in the same league as Ty Cobb (see no. 10). Therefore, even though Speaker compiled high batting averages of .383, .362, and .352, he won the American League batting title only once in 1916, with a .386 average. Speaker's specialty was hitting doubles. He led the league eight times in two-baggers, and his 792 lifetime doubles still tops the all-time list. His lifetime batting average is a sparkling .344.

As great a hitter as Speaker was, his hitting was almost overshadowed by his defensive play. He had great speed and an ability to go back on a ball hit deeply. Unlike most outfielders of his day, Speaker played very shallow. He constantly charged in to catch sinking line drives and pop flies before they dropped to become base hits. Many youngsters began imitating Speaker's defensive style, and outfield play was revolutionized.

After a bitter salary dispute, Speaker was traded to the Cleveland Indians for $50,000 following the 1915 season. In 1919, he became Cleveland's player-manager, and he led them to a World Series championship in 1920.

Speaker abruptly resigned as player-manager of the Indians following the 1926 season, and it was rumored that he was about to be implicated in an alleged plot with Ty Cobb to fix a game between Cleveland and Detroit back in 1919. However, both players were cleared by the Commissioner's office, and Speaker played for two more seasons with the Washington Senators. He was inducted into the Hall of Fame in 1937.

One of the most colorful personalities ever to brighten the world of baseball, **CASEY STENGEL** was also one of the most successful managers in the game's history.

Charles Dillon Stengel was born in 1890 in Kansas City, Missouri, and broke into the majors as a player with the Brooklyn Dodgers in 1912. He also played with the Pittsburgh Pirates, Boston Braves, and New York Giants during an unspectacular, but solid career. He hit over .300 three times, and his lifetime average was .284. In addition, he hit a sparkling .393, with 11 doubles and 2 home runs in three World Series in the 1920s.

Finished as a player after the 1925 season, Stengel became a manager of several minor league teams along with the Dodgers and Braves of the major league. Stengel had a rather undistinguished career. In nine years as a major league skipper, he never finished higher than fifth place.

In 1948, Stengel finally did win a pennant, as manager of the Oakland club in the New York Yankees farm system. The following year, he was promoted to manager of the Yankees, and because of his lackluster record, the reaction in the world of baseball was sheer disbelief.

Stengel quickly proved, however, that he could handle New York's roster of veteran stars and talented youngsters. In 1949, he won the pennant by one game over the Boston Red Sox, and then went on to beat the Brooklyn Dodgers in the World Series. The Yankees then won four more pennants in a row, as well as four consecutive World Series. No one had ever done that before in baseball history.

Stengel went on to win ten pennants and seven World Series during the twelve years he managed the Yankees—an unmatched record of success. Because of the Yankees' deep and powerful bench, he perfected the art of "platooning," alternating different players at the same position, depending upon the opposing pitcher.

In 1960, the Yankees fired Stengel because, at age seventy, they believed he was too old. Two years later he resurfaced as manager of the New York Mets and took it all with a smile as the Mets were setting all-time records for losing.

Throughout his career, Stengel was a favorite with both the press and the fans. He used a type of double-talk, dubbed "Stengelese," in which the truth was usually buried in a mountain of seemingly non-related verbiage, such as: "The secret of managing is to keep the guys who hate you away from the guys who are undecided."

Elected to the Hall of Fame in 1966, Stengel was named baseball's greatest manager during its centennial celebration in 1969.

Although his career was seriously affected by health problems, **GEORGE SISLER** was one of the greatest first basemen of all time.

Born in Manchester, Ohio, Sisler was a sensational high school athlete. He signed a contract with the Akron team of the Ohio-Pennsylvania League that was to take effect on graduation day. However, Sisler then turned around and enrolled at the University of Michigan, where he played under Branch Rickey.

After a brilliant college career, Sisler signed a contract with the St. Louis Browns, for whom Rickey was then manager. In the meantime, Sisler's Akron contract had been purchased by the Pittsburgh Pirates. With both the Browns and Pirates claiming him as their player, they appealed to the three-member National Commission, which governed baseball at the time, to settle the issue. After much debate, the Commission awarded Sisler to the Browns, ruling that he was a minor when he had signed the Akron contract.

Sisler joined the Browns in 1915 and began his career as a pitcher. During his first year, he posted a record of 4–4. He also played 66 games at first base and in the outfield and demonstrated promise as a hitter.

Deciding that Sisler had more of a future as a hitter, the Browns made him their regular first baseman. That year he hit .305.

After three more seasons batting in the .340s and .350s, the left-handed hitter led the American League with a .407 mark in 1920. He also collected 257 hits—a single-season record that still stands. Two years later, Sisler again cracked the .400 barrier, hitting an amazing .420. He led the league with 246 hits, 134 runs, 18 triples, and 51 stolen bases, and struck out only fourteen times in nearly 600 at-bats.

Although Sisler's hitting received all the attention, his fielding was considered superb. He was smooth around first base with excellent range and led the American League first basemen in assists six times.

After the 1922 season, Sisler developed double vision stemming from infected sinuses. An operation failed to remedy the problem, and he missed the entire 1923 season. He returned to the Browns as player-manager in 1924, and dropped off considerably, hitting "only" .305 that year. While his health problems almost certainly prevented him from regaining the form he once had, Sisler was still a very solid player. He bounced back to hit .345 in 1925, and after dipping to .290 in 1926, he hit .325 or better for the next three seasons.

Sisler retired after the 1930 season with a .340 lifetime batting average. He was elected to the Hall of Fame in 1939.

◆ **BABE RUTH** was—and quite possibly still is—the greatest player in baseball history.

Born in Baltimore, Maryland, George Herman "Babe" Ruth was wild as a young man. He was sent to a reform school and orphanage, where he learned many of the baseball skills that would make him a legend.

Ruth came up to the majors as a pitcher in 1914 with the Boston Red Sox of the American League. Over the next six seasons, Ruth became one of Boston's star hurlers, winning 20 games twice, and helping the Red Sox to World Series victories in 1916 and 1918. Ruth also showed talent as a hitter, and in 1918, he played almost half the season in the outfield or at first base. The next year, he became nearly a full-time position player and led the league in home runs, runs, RBIs, and slugging averages.

Red Sox owner and Broadway producer Harry Frazee needed money, though, and after the Red Sox had a poor season in

1919, he sold Ruth's contract to the New York Yankees for $100,000.

With the Yankees, Ruth was strictly a hitter—and what a hitter he was. In 1920, he hit 54 homers, far surpassing any other American League team. Over the next fourteen seasons, he won nine more home run titles, led the league in slugging average ten times, and knocked in more than 130 runs nine times.

Ruth also completely turned the Yankees' fortunes around. The team won seven pennants and four world championships while he played for them. He and Lou Gehrig (see no. 26) make up the most feared one-two punch in baseball.

However, the real measure of Ruth's greatness extends beyond stats. His booming homers made high scoring popular and completely revolutionized the game from the low-scoring, dead-ball era. In addition, he single-handedly breathed new life into a sport that had lost public favor after the infamous 1919 "Black Sox" scandal. No other athlete has ever had such profound influence on a sport like Ruth.

Throughout his career, Ruth made almost as many headlines off the field as he did on it. At various times, he ran afoul of his manager, who fined and suspended him, and the baseball commissioner, who also suspended him. He also lived a high life filled with frequent overindulgences in food, alcohol, and romantic escapades. And yet, through it all, he remained the most wildly popular athlete of his era—particularly with children, who worshipped him and whom he treated with great affection and attention.

After fourteen seasons with the Yankees, Ruth spent his last season with the Boston Braves in the National League. He was one of the first five players elected to the Hall of Fame.

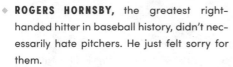

◆ **ROGERS HORNSBY,** the greatest right-handed hitter in baseball history, didn't necessarily hate pitchers. He just felt sorry for them.

With a fiery personality that infuriated both opposing players and teammates, Hornsby cut a wide swath through the National League in the 1920s and set new marks for batting excellence.

Rogers Hornsby was born in 1896, in Winters, Texas. His unusual first name came from his mother, whose maiden name was Rogers. She was a big baseball fan and encouraged him in his desire to play, even though he initially didn't show much promise. However, the St. Louis Cardinals were impressed enough by the skinny infielder's dedication to the sport that they took a chance on him and paid a club in Hugo, Oklahoma, $500 for his contract.

After a so-so rookie year in 1916, the brash Hornsby matured rapidly by leading the National League in slugging percentage in his second season in the majors. His batting average of .327 ranked second in the league.

Beginning with the 1920 season, when he moved to second base permanently, Hornsby blossomed into a peerless right-handed hitter. That year, he hit .370, the highest average by a National League second baseman in the twentieth century. It also began a string of six consecutive batting titles for Hornsby.

Not expected to duplicate his success the following year, Hornsby bettered it, hitting .397 with 126 runs batted in. He followed that up with a .401 average in 1922, and then in 1924, he had his highest average ever, hitting an astonishing .424—another twentieth-century National League record. He averaged over .400 from 1920 to 1925 and hit below .361 just once during the entire decade. He also led the league eight times in slugging average, four times in hits and RBIs, and twice in home runs.

Hornsby's keen batting eye was legendary. He didn't read the newspaper or go to the movies, claiming they were strains on the eyes. His dedication to the game was frightening. In 1926, he postponed his mother's funeral so it wouldn't interfere with his participation in the World Series.

However, as good a player as Hornsby was, he was not liked much by teammates or opponents. He traveled prolifically during his career because of his brash and outspoken personality, playing with the St. Louis Cardinals, the Boston Braves, the Chicago Cubs, the New York Giants, and the St. Louis Browns. After he retired, he managed several clubs but was repeatedly fired because he failed to get along with either the owners or many of the players.

Hornsby's lifetime .358 average is second only to Ty Cobb's. He was elected to the Hall of Fame in 1942.

A four-sport star athlete in college, **FRANKIE FRISCH** was coaxed into playing major league baseball by Giants manager John McGraw, and he became a spark plug and a leader on the great Giants teams of the 1920s.

Frisch was a New York City boy through and through. Born in the Bronx in 1898, he was the captain of the baseball, basketball, and football teams at Fordham University, and he also starred in track. McGraw was alerted to Frisch's potential by Fordham's baseball coach and offered him a minor league contract. However, Frisch turned it down until McGraw sweetened his offer to a major league deal. He joined the New York Giants in 1919, and by 1920, he was the team's regular second baseman.

Frisch was the final ingredient for success for the Giants, who reeled off four straight pennants from 1921 to 1924 and two world championships in 1921 and 1922. Over those four years, Frisch hit .341, .327, .348, and .328.

In the 1922 World Series victory over the New York Yankees, Frisch hit a blistering .471.

Nicknamed "The Fordham Flash" because of his speed, Frisch led the National League in steals with 49 in 1921, 48 in 1927, and 28 in 1931. In an era when the steal was declining as an offensive weapon, Frisch was one of the main base bandits of his generation, stealing a grand total of 419 bases during his career.

From 1921 to 1931, Frisch never hit less than .300. Some baseball experts credit Frisch with being the first power-hitting switch-hitter. A natural left-handed batter, Frisch was fooling around one day as a righty. McGraw saw this and urged him to give switch-hitting a try. He hit 105 homers in his career.

However, Frisch and McGraw didn't always see eye to eye, and in 1927, Frisch was traded to the St. Louis Cardinals for Rogers Hornsby. Frisch again proved to be just what a team needed to win the pennant. He helped the famous "Gashouse Gang" team win pennants in 1928 and 1930, and the pennant and world championship in 1931. Highly respected for his fielding prowess, hitting skills, and competitive fire, Frisch also won the National League's Most Valuable Player (MVP) Award in 1931.

In 1933, Frisch was named player-manager of the Cardinals, and the next year, he led the team to another pennant and a seven-game World Series victory over the Detroit Tigers. He retired in 1937 with a career batting average of .316 and a whopping 2,880 hits.

After his playing career ended, Frisch worked briefly as a baseball radio broadcaster before returning to managing in the 1940s with the Pittsburgh Pirates and, later, the Chicago Cubs.

A seventeen-year major leaguer—all spent with the Pittsburgh Pirates—**PIE TRAYNOR** was at one time considered the best all-around third baseman ever to play the game.

Harold Joseph Traynor was born in Framingham, Massachusetts, and was the son of a printer. He earned his nickname "Pie" because he was excessively fond of his mother's homemade pies.

Traynor was a standout in sandlot ball, and in 1918, he tried to get a tryout with the low-performing Boston Braves of the National League. However, the Braves, who could have used all the help they could get at the time, turned him down.

Undaunted, Traynor signed with Portsmouth of the Virginia League in 1920. His play was so impressive that the Pittsburgh Pirates signed him. After playing briefly with the Pirates in 1920 and 1921, he went up to the majors for good in 1922. At first, the Pirates put him at shortstop, and Traynor floundered. Then they moved him to third base, and a future Hall of Famer was born.

After batting .282 in his rookie season, Traynor slammed the ball at a .338 clip the following season. This began a string of seasons in which Traynor hit .317 or better seven out of eight years. In one four-season stretch, from 1927 to 1930, his batting average never fell below .337. All told, Traynor hit over .300 for ten years out of his seventeen-year career, compiling a lifetime .320 batting average.

Pittsburgh won two pennants during Traynor's career. In 1925, they beat the Washington Senators in the World Series, with Traynor hitting .346. In 1927, however, when the Pirates were swept by the "Murderer's Row" New York Yankees, he only managed a .200 average.

Traynor was also quite solid in the field, particularly with balls hit down the line. He also had excellent range to his left and could charge bunts well. Extremely popular with the Pittsburgh fans, he was a logical choice to become player-manager of the team in 1934. Later that season, he broke his right arm in a slide home, which seriously curtailed his playing days. He retired in 1937 and was replaced as manager during the 1939 season.

However, Traynor continued to maintain strong ties to the organization. He later became a scout for Pittsburgh, and then was the team's radio announcer for more than twenty years.

During the second half of the twentieth century, players such as Brooks Robinson and Mike Schmidt supplanted Traynor as top all-around third basemen in the eyes of many. However, Traynor was still the top player at his position in his era. He was elected to the Hall of Fame in 1948.

LEWIS ROBERT "HACK" WILSON was hardly built like a classic baseball player—a fireplug of a man, he had a huge barrel chest and tree trunk legs on a five-foot-six body, with size six feet. Yet, during his twelve-year major league career, he was one of the most feared sluggers in the National League.

Wilson was born in Elwood City, Pennsylvania. School wasn't something Wilson enjoyed, so he began working at an early age. He developed his tremendous upper body strength by swinging heavy hammers in a nearby locomotive works company.

Wilson got the nickname "Hack" because of his resemblance to George Hackenschmidt, a well-known wrestler and weightlifter from the early twentieth century.

In 1921, Wilson began playing baseball professionally. However, even though he hit better than .350 for three years in the minors, most major league clubs didn't wish to take a risk on him because they thought

he was too short. However, the five-foot-seven Giants manager John McGraw didn't have a problem with his height, so Wilson signed with the New York club.

After two years as a part-time player with the Giants, in 1924 and 1925, Wilson was sent down to the minors and left unprotected. The Chicago Cubs grabbed him out of the Giants farm system and stardom found Hack Wilson.

For the next six seasons with the Cubs, Wilson was one of the best home run hitters in baseball; he led the National League four times and smashed a total of 190 during that time. He led the Cubs into the World Series in 1929 with 39 homers, 159 runs batted in, and a .345 average. His best year came in 1930, when he hit .356, belted 56 homers, and drove in 191 runs. His home run total was the league record until Mark McGwire (see no. 95) broke it in 1998. To this day, Wilson's RBI mark is still the all-time major league record for a single season.

Sadly, 1930 was Wilson's last good season. For years, he had had a drinking problem, and alcohol finally took a toll on his skills. After his average slumped to .261 in 1931, the Cubs traded him to the Brooklyn Dodgers. He rebounded the next year by hitting .297, but his performance on the diamond went steadily downhill after that. By 1935, he was out of baseball. He ended his career with a .307 lifetime average and 244 homers.

After he left baseball, Wilson worked a series of odd jobs and continued to drink. He died in Baltimore, Maryland, in 1948. In 1979, he was elected to the Hall of Fame.

The most dominant catcher of his era, **GABBY HARTNETT** had an outstanding twenty-year National League career and hit one of the most famous home runs of all time.

He was born Charles Leo Hartnett in Woonsocket, Rhode Island, in 1900. One of fourteen children to a streetcar conductor and semipro catcher father, young Charles was soon taken under his father's wing and taught everything about catching. While he was working in a steel mill, Hartnett played semipro ball. He signed with the Worcester, Massachusetts, team and attracted the attention of pro scouts. Although the New York Giants had an opportunity to sign him, they passed him up because they thought his hands were too small for a catcher. However, the Chicago Cubs liked what they saw and acquired him in 1922.

Hartnett developed slowly as a catcher, as many players in that position do. He was not ready to become the Cubs' full-time backstop until 1924, but once he took over the position, he held onto it and remained the team's primary catcher until 1940.

When Hartnett became the regular catcher for the Cubs, he hit .299. Thereafter he averaged around .275 until 1930, when he exploded with a .339 average, 37 homers, and 122 RBIs. He also led the National League in putouts, assists, and fielding averages. After several solid but unspectacular seasons, Hartnett had another breakout year in 1935. He won the league's Most Valuable Player (MVP) Award, hitting .344 with 13 homers, 91 RBIs, and led all National League receivers in assists, double plays, and fielding averages.

Affable, durable, and an excellent defensive catcher, Hartnett was nicknamed "Gabby" by a Chicago sportswriter because he constantly chatted with opposing hitters when he was behind the plate.

Hartnett was on four Chicago pennant winners in 1929, 1932, 1935, and 1938, yet each time, they failed to win the World Series. Hartnett's famous homer came in 1938 against the Pittsburgh Pirates, when the Chicago Cubs were half a game behind the Pirates for the pennant. With two outs in the bottom of the ninth inning and darkness rapidly approaching, Hartnett smashed a home run to give the Cubs the flag. His "homer in the gloaming" was the most famous blast in National League history until Bobby Thompson's won the pennant for the New York Giants in 1951.

When his playing days were winding down, Hartnett became player-manager for the Cubs, displaying the same easygoing temperament he exhibited as a player. He spent his final season as a player and a coach for the New York Giants in 1941 and hit .300.

Hartnett was inducted into the Hall of Fame in 1955.

For a young man with a lot of talent, it sure took **"LEFTY" GROVE** a long time to make it to the major leagues. But once he got there, it wasn't long before he proved that he belonged near the very top of the game's best players.

Robert Moses Grove was born in Lonaconing, Maryland, in 1900. He worked as a glassblower, miner, and railroad hand before deciding that he might have a better future in baseball.

Grove broke into professional baseball at the age of twenty and spent more than four years in the minors, where he won 109 games and lost only 36. Finally, after the 1924 season, Connie Mack (see no. 1) of the Philadelphia A's purchased Grove's contract from the minor league Baltimore Orioles for $100,600. The extra $600 was to make the deal worth more than the $100,000 that the Yankees had paid the Red Sox for Babe Ruth a few years earlier.

Grove soon proved worth it. After

conquering control problems his first two seasons, he put together seven consecutive seasons winning 20 games or more, including a career high 31 victories in 1931. During that time, he was the ace of the A's staff and helped lead the team to three straight pennants from 1929 to 1931 and two World Series titles.

With a blazing fastball and sharp breaking curve that he added later, the left-handed Grove won 300 games during his career while losing just 141. He led the league with his earned run average (ERA) nine times, in strikeouts seven times, and in winning percentage five times. In 1931, he received the Baseball Writer's Association's first American League Most Valuable Player (MVP) Award. Grove was so fast that one sportswriter said he could "throw a lamb chop past a wolf." He also had a very durable arm. Although he was mainly a starting pitcher, Grove often pitched in relief. In 1930, when he won 28 games, he started 32 and completed 22. He also pitched 18 games in relief and led the league with nine saves.

Grove was a fierce competitor who had a habit of tearing his clothes and smashing lockers when he lost. He would also throw balls at his own teammates in batting practice if he thought they were crowding the plate or hitting him too well.

In 1934, Connie Mack, losing money and desperate to cut his payroll, sold Grove's contract to the Boston Red Sox for $125,000. Although his fastball had lost a little steam by then, he still won more than 100 games for the Red Sox in eight seasons.

Grove retired in 1941 and was elected to the Hall of Fame in 1947.

Despite having one of the most unorthodox batting styles of any player of his era, **AL SIMMONS** was one of the most outstanding hitters in baseball history.

Baseball enthusiasts always give the same advice to young right-handed hitters coming up—step toward the pitcher as you begin your swing and never step toward third base. That latter movement has been compared to stepping into an imaginary bucket alongside the batter's box. According to conventional wisdom, a hitter can't be effective if he is "bailing out."

However, that is exactly what Al Simmons did. He was a sensational hitter during the 1920s and 1930s with his front foot pointed firmly at third base. Earning the nickname "Bucketfoot Al," he didn't care how odd he looked at the plate. He just kept lashing out base hits and laughing at the experts.

He was born Aloysius Harry Szymanski in Milwaukee, Wisconsin, in 1902. After starring for two years in the minors, Simmons signed with the Philadelphia A's of the American League in 1924.

In his first season, Simmons hit .308 with 102 runs batted in. In 1925, he batted .384 and led the league with 253 hits, which is still the all-time single season record for a right-handed hitter. That year he also drove home 129 runs to become the first player in league history to drive in over 100 runs in his first two seasons.

The A's manager, Connie Mack (see no. 1), who had dismantled his first great team in the mid-1910s because of financial difficulties, was now building a second great team, and Simmons became a vital piece of the puzzle.

From 1929 to 1931, the A's won three consecutive pennants and two world championships. In those three seasons, Simmons batted .365, .381, and .390, respectively—the last two figures winning him two batting titles in a row. In their three World Series bids, Simmons hit .300, .364, and .333.

Besides his hitting, Simmons was a superb outfielder. He had good range, and his strong throwing arm threw out many runners trying to take an extra base on his watch.

When Mack began to break up his second great team in 1933, again because of financial difficulties, Simmons was sent to the Chicago White Sox. Over the next several years, he played for several different teams until age slowed down his bat. Finally, he retired after the 1944 season. He finished with 2,927 hits—just 73 short of the magical 3,000 mark—and a lifetime .334 batting average.

In the late 1940s, when age reduced Mack's effectiveness, Simmons returned to the A's as a coach and an unofficial manager. Simmons was elected to the Hall of Fame in 1953.

A hero and true legend, **LOU GEHRIG**'s story transcends baseball and indeed all of sports.

Henry Louis Gehrig was born in New York City in 1903 and was an all-sports star at Commerce High School. His talent won him a baseball and football scholarship to Columbia University.

Gehrig played baseball only as a freshman, but the New York Yankees, who had scouted him, were impressed, and they signed him to a contract.

After two years in the minors, Gehrig went up to the Yankees in 1925 ready to be their first baseman. Initially, though, Gehrig rode the bench. But on June 2, 1925, the regular Yankee first baseman, Wally Pipp, was given the day off because of a headache. When his backup also couldn't play, Gehrig was tapped in. It would be almost fourteen years before he ever sat out again.

That first year, Gehrig hit .295 with 68 runs batted in. Then, over the next dozen seasons, he racked up hitting statistics that

were nothing short of astounding. His RBI totals were awesome with an American League record of 184 in 1931 and other great season totals of 175, 174, 165, and 159. And his batting averages were just as impressive: .374, .373, .363, and his career-high .379 in 1930. In addition, in seven World Series, he hit .361 with 35 RBIs as he helped lead the Yankees to six world titles.

Unfortunately for Gehrig, he played much of his career in the larger-than-life shadow of Babe Ruth, who was more colorful and flamboyant compared to the quiet and reserved Gehrig. Still, Gehrig's teammates and ardent baseball fans everywhere knew how important he was to the Yankees' success during the 1920s and 1930s. Season after season, he played every game—2,130 straight—earning his famous nickname, "The Iron Horse."

Gehrig finally tailed off in the 1938 season, but it wasn't until spring training the next year when both he and his teammates noticed something was terribly wrong. He began the year in a slump and was even having trouble in the field. On May 2, 1939, he took himself out of the lineup. Shortly thereafter, he learned that he was suffering from a rare illness called amyotrophic lateral sclerosis, known commonly as ALS or Lou Gehrig's disease, for which there was no cure.

On July 4, 1939, the Yankees held a day honoring Gehrig, when he made his famous statement that despite the "bad break" he had been given, he considered himself "the luckiest man on the face of the Earth."

The Hall of Fame waived its usual waiting period and inducted him immediately in 1939. Two years later, this special man and baseball immortal died.

TONY LAZZERI was the heavy-hitting second baseman on many of the great New York Yankee teams of the late 1920s and 1930s. He was also involved in one of the most fabled "showdowns" in World Series history.

A San Francisco native, Lazzeri got his start in professional baseball in the early 1920s, but there was no indication that he would become one of the hardest-hitting second basemen in American League history. Then, in 1925, he had a sensational year with the Salt Lake City Bees of the Pacific Coast League. That year, Lazzeri hit 60 homers with a mind-boggling 222 RBIs. The Yankees signed him for $75,000 after that incredible season.

New York Yankees manager Miller Huggins was seeking to revitalize the team's offense in 1926, and Lazzeri did his part by batting .275 with 114 RBIs, making second in the league. Over the next ten seasons, Lazzeri drove in more than 100 runs seven times. He also hit a good average as well, earning a high batting mark of .354 in 1929. He got his nickname "Poosh 'Em Up" for his ability to deliver clutch hits with men on base.

Lazzeri's big bat contributed mightily to the Yankees' achievements in the late 1920s and 1930s. With him on second base, the team won seven pennants and six World Series titles.

However, despite all that success, Lazzeri is probably most famous for one failure. In the seventh game of the 1926 World Series against the St. Louis Cardinals, St. Louis was clinging to a one-run lead in the seventh inning. The Yankees had bases loaded, two out, and Lazzeri coming up. The Cardinals brought in the great but aging pitcher, Grover Cleveland Alexander—who had thrown a complete game victory over the Yankees the day before—to pitch in relief.

After hitting a long drive that was nearly a grand slam homer but went foul, Lazzeri struck out. Alexander then finished the game in relief to clinch the Series for St. Louis. The confrontation between the two men has become legendary in baseball history, particularly because Alexander was allegedly nursing a hangover.

After the 1937 season, Lazzeri left the Yankees for the Chicago Cubs, and he helped them win the National League pennant in 1938. However, his skills had begun to diminish, and after being traded twice in 1939, he retired at the end of the season.

Lazzeri was elected to the Hall of Fame in 1991.

Although his career was shortened by a near-fatal beaning—or being hit in the head by a ball, often intentionally, to cause injury—**MICKEY COCHRANE** is still considered one of the greatest catchers in baseball history.

Gordon Stanley Cochrane was born in Bridgewater, Massachusetts, in 1903. At Boston University, he was a member of the baseball, football, basketball, and track teams.

After he graduated, he joined a minor league baseball team in Delaware. Once behind the plate, his raw natural ability attracted the attention of the Philadelphia A's leader Connie Mack (see no. 1). He was so certain of Cochrane's talent that he took over the minor league Portland Beavers team in the Pacific Coast League so that Cochrane would have a place to hone his skills without the risk of the A's losing him to another club.

By 1925, Mack felt that Cochrane was ready to play in the majors and brought him

up to the A's. That year, he caught a rookie record of 134 games and hit .331. He hit more than .300 nine times in thirteen seasons and caught more than 120 games in each of his first ten seasons.

Cochrane's best years with the A's were from 1929 to 1931. He hit .331, .357, and .349, respectively, in those years, while helping to lead the A's to three straight pennants and two World Series triumphs. He operated to perfection a pitching staff that included the immortal Lefty Grove (see no. 24). An intense player, Cochrane was known as "Black Mike" for the foul moods he exhibited when things didn't go his team's way.

During the Great Depression in the 1930s, Mack began to sell off some of his best players. After the 1933 season, he sent Cochrane to the Detroit Tigers for $100,000. There, as a player-manager, Cochrane had an immediate impact, leading Detroit to the pennant in 1934 and the pennant and world championship in 1935, while hitting .320 and .319, respectively.

On May 25, 1937, Cochrane was beaned by New York Yankee pitcher Bump Hadley. He suffered a triple skull fracture, and doctors only gave him a fifty-fifty chance of survival. For the next few days, Cochrane hovered on the brink of delirium and death, one time ordering his wife to "get him a new head."

Although he eventually recovered and wanted to return to the field, Tigers owner Walter Briggs would not allow it because doctors said another beaning could prove fatal. His playing career ruled over after thirteen seasons, Cochrane managed Detroit one more year and then left the game.

He retired as baseball's best hitting catcher, with an average of .320 and a .419 on-base percentage. He was inducted into the Hall of Fame in 1947.

◆ If it wasn't for a bad decision by the Detroit Tigers and legendary outfielder Ty Cobb, **CARL HUBBELL** might never have become a great pitcher with the New York Giants.

Hubbell was born in Carthage, Missouri, and grew up on a pecan farm in Oklahoma. In 1925, he was pitching for the Oklahoma City Indians of the Western League when his contract was sold to the major league Tigers. Cobb and the Tigers took one look at Hubbell throwing his screwball—his signature "reverse curve" that breaks in on left-handed batters and away from righties—and told him to forget it. They said that he would never make it in the major leagues with that crazy pitch and would hurt his arm in the process. Hubbell, who had posted a record of 17–13 with Oklahoma City using the screwball, took their advice. He discarded the pitch and thereafter threw so badly that the Tigers gave up on him entirely in 1928.

After that, Hubbell drifted to the Texas League. It was there that Giants scout Dick Kinsella saw him and told Giants manager John McGraw about him. McGraw had no problem with the screwball, and he signed Hubbell in July 1928. The pitcher promptly won 10 games for the Giants that year.

Hubbell followed up his 10-victory rookie season by winning 18 games in 1929. However, it was from 1933 to 1937 that "King Carl" dominated the game as baseball's best pitcher. He won 23, 21, 23, 26, and 22 games, respectively, during those years, while pitching the Giants to the World Series in 1933, 1936, and 1937. The Giants won the world championship in 1933, and Hubbell won two games in that World Series.

Hubbell is perhaps most famous for striking out five of the greatest hitters in history in a row in the 1934 All-Star Game: Babe Ruth, Lou Gehrig, Jimmie Foxx, Al Simmons, and Joe Cronin. His dominating performance caused National League All-Star catcher Gabby Hartnett to yell over at the American League dugout, "We gotta look at that all season."

Known as "The Meal Ticket," Hubbell won the National League's Most Valuable Player (MVP) Award in 1933 and 1936. In 1936, he ended the season with 16 straight wins, and when he won his first eight games of 1937, he set a major league record of twenty-four consecutive regular season victories. Over the course of his career, Hubbell won 253 games.

However, throwing the screwball did damage his arm, and although Hubbell underwent elbow surgery after the 1938 season, he was never the same pitcher. He retired after the 1943 season and was elected to the Hall of Fame in 1947.

◆ **COOL PAPA BELL** was perhaps the fastest player in baseball history. However, because he played his entire career in the Negro Leagues, his speed and talents remain less known to many.

James Thomas Bell was born in Starkville, Mississippi, in 1903. He played Black semipro baseball before joining the St. Louis Stars of the Negro National League in 1922 as a pitcher who threw a wicked curveball and a fade-away knuckleball. However, when he beat one of the fastest players in Negro baseball in a footrace, Bell was moved to center field.

Bell received his unusual nickname as a young player, when he seemed undaunted playing before large crowds. When just "cool" seemed inadequate, "papa" was added, and a legend was born.

Center field at Stars' Park was extremely deep—about 500 feet. Bell patrolled the outfield there for ten seasons, hauling in long drives hit by opposing batters into the deep power alleys.

Like all Negro League players, Bell's extraordinary skills came to light when he played exhibition games against white major leaguers. Once, in 1931, Bell singled to open the game, then stole second, third, and home. This ignited the Stars to an 18–3 victory. One of the white all-stars remarked that Bell was like a "Black Ty Cobb."

"You're wrong," said future Hall-of-Famer Lloyd Waner, watching Bell scamper around the bases. "Cobb is like a white Bell." Stories abound about Bell's blazing speed. Former Negro League players swore that if Bell hit a ball to the left side of the infield and it took more than one bounce, it was impossible to throw him out.

After his tenure with the Stars ended in 1931, Bell played with the Detroit Wolves and Pittsburgh Crawfords, among other teams. In addition, like other Black stars, he played winter ball in Cuba and Mexico nearly every year.

In 1933, Bell had perhaps his greatest season, hitting .379 in around 200 games with a reported 175 stolen bases—a figure that has never been approached by any other ballplayer. However, due to variations in season length and record keeping for Negro League games, the exact final total is unknown.

Bell retired with a lifetime batting average of .338, and a .395 average in exhibition games against white major leaguers. If Black players had not been barred from major league baseball before 1947, Bell might have set some unparalleled base-stealing records.

Bell was elected to the Hall of Fame in 1974.

People called **CHARLIE GEHRINGER** "The Mechanical Man" because he went out year after year without fanfare, fielded his second base position flawlessly, and compiled a .300-plus batting average—just like a machine.

"He says hello on opening day and good-bye on closing day, and in between, he hits .350," said his manager, Mickey Cochrane.

Gehringer was born in Fowlerville, Michigan, the son of a chicken farmer. After helping with the chores, young Charlie decided that his future was in baseball, not with chickens. He attended the University of Michigan on a baseball scholarship, and in 1924, he tried out for the Detroit Tigers, who were then being managed by the great Ty Cobb (see no. 10). Cobb quickly signed him.

After a few seasons in the minors, Gehringer became the Tigers' regular second baseman at the beginning of the 1926 season. He remained a fixture at that position until 1942.

Gehringer hit .277 in his first season in the majors. Over the next fifteen years, he hit .300 or better every year except in 1932, when he finished at .298. He had a spectacular season in 1929, when he hit .339 and led the league in several offensive categories: hits with 215, runs scored with 131, doubles with 45, triples with 19, and stolen bases with 28.

Not only was Gehringer a consistent hitter he was also a sensational fielder who had a knack of making even the hardest plays look easy. He led the American League in fielding percentage for second basemen seven times.

Gehringer helped lead the Tigers to three pennants and one world championship. His remarkable consistency also extended into his World Series play. His average for the three Series he played in—1934, 1935, and

1940—was .321, one point higher than his lifetime batting average.

Gehringer was often so quiet and unassuming that even his teammates were surprised at his excellence. Detroit slugger and teammate Hank Greenberg told one story that illustrated Gehringer's low-key demeanor.

"I had my best season in 1937," Greenberg said, "with 40 homers and 183 RBIs. The newsmen always wrote about me in every town we went to. Then, the year ended, I looked up, and Charlie had hit .371 and had won the league's Most Valuable Player (MVP)."

Gehringer retired after the 1942 season, when he felt he could no longer perform at the level he desired. During the 1950s, Gehringer joined the Tigers' front office, first as general manager and then as vice president. He was elected to the Hall of Fame in 1949.

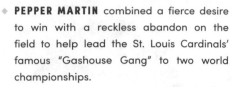

PEPPER MARTIN combined a fierce desire to win with a reckless abandon on the field to help lead the St. Louis Cardinals' famous "Gashouse Gang" to two world championships.

John Leonard Roosevelt Martin was born in Temple, Oklahoma, in 1904. He first went up to the Cardinals in 1928, hitting .308 in 39 games. After spending most of the next two years in the minors, he returned to the Cardinals for good in 1931. That year, he hit an even .300 with 16 stolen bases in 123 games and helped spark the team to their second straight National League pennant.

However, it was his performance in the 1931 World Series that earned Martin the legendary nickname "The Wild Horse of the Osage." Martin hit .500, including a homer and five RBIs, and stole five bases to ignite the Cardinals to a seven-game upset of the favored Philadelphia A's. Martin's destruction of the vaunted A's pitching staff was so great that a sportswriter for the

New York Sun wrote that he had just seen a World Series between "the A's and one John Leonard Martin of Oklahoma."

After an injury limited his play in 1932, Martin came back strong the next season. He hit .316 and led the league in runs scored with 122 and stolen bases with 26. That year, Martin played the entire season on third base, after having first come up to the Cardinals as an outfielder. Thereafter, he alternated between playing third and outfield for the rest of his career.

In 1934, Martin again led the league in stolen bases and had another outstanding World Series as the Cardinals bounced back from a disappointing season the previous year to win the world championship once again.

Despite his size at just five foot eight and 170 pounds, Martin was a wild man on the field. His uniform was always dirty and often torn because of the way he played. While he wasn't exceptionally fast, he terrorized opponents by throwing himself wildly into bases and fielders.

A vibrant personality, Martin liked to have fun. Once, when the temperature soared to 110 degrees Fahrenheit during a game, he and teammate Dizzy Dean built a fire in front of the dugout and sat in front of it wrapped in blankets.

Martin batted .298 during his twelve-year career with St. Louis, leading the league in steals three times. Fans loved Martin's intense style of running, which he never abandoned. At age fifty, managing in the minor leagues, Martin sent himself in as a pinch hitter, singled, then stretched it into a triple with a belly flop slide into third base.

Fiery and controversial, **LEO DUROCHER** surpassed a mediocre playing career by becoming a Hall-of-Fame manager.

Folks in West Springfield, Massachusetts, where Durocher was born and grew up, remembered him as a ball-playing youngster who was always chattering and wise-cracking—he apparently earned his nickname "Leo the Lip" from his earliest days. As a young man, Durocher played with numerous semipro teams until he finally landed with Hartford Senators of the Eastern League in 1925. Later that year, the New York Yankees purchased Durocher's contract for $7,000.

Durocher played two full seasons for the Yankees in 1928 and 1929, dividing his time between second base and shortstop. He was a good fielder, but not much of a hitter. In a seventeen-year career that saw him also play for the Cincinnati Reds, St. Louis Cardinals, and Brooklyn Dodgers, he only ever hit .247. Although his batting may have been weak, Durocher had a combative personality. He wouldn't give in to anybody, and he believed in criticizing friends and foe alike.

In 1939, Durocher became the player-manager of the Dodgers. The team had long been an also-ran in the National League, but Durocher instilled his fiery spirit in them. In 1941, he led Brooklyn to its first pennant in twenty years, although they lost the World Series to the Yankees in five games.

Durocher retired as a player in 1945 but continued as the Dodger skipper. Both in and out of uniform, he always enjoyed being the center of attention. When off the field, he was often seen at the racetrack or out on the town with his beautiful wife, movie star Laraine Day. It was that high-living lifestyle that got Durocher suspended in 1947 by Commissioner Happy Chandler for conduct detrimental to baseball. As a result, even though Durocher had been supportive of the Dodgers' decision to sign Jackie Robinson and break baseball's color line, he wasn't able to manage Robinson during his first season in the major league.

Durocher returned in 1948, but halfway through the season, he stunned the baseball world by jumping to manage the Dodgers' bitter rival, the New York Giants. With the Giants, Durocher won two pennants—in 1951, when they defeated Brooklyn in a playoff on Bobby Thomson's famous home run, and in 1954, when they beat the heavily favored Cleveland Indians to win the World Series. Durocher also took under his wing a struggling rookie named Willie Mays and convinced him that he was going to be the Giants' permanent center fielder.

Later on, Durocher also managed the Chicago Cubs and the Houston Astros. He retired as a manager with more than 2,000 victories across twenty-four major league seasons. He was elected to the Hall of Fame in 1994.

"Don't look back. Something might be gaining on you," advised the seemingly ageless **SATCHEL PAIGE**, in one of his six rules for staying young. It's obvious that, over his career spanning several decades, which made him the most popular pitcher in the Negro Leagues, Paige followed his own advice.

Much of his career and his life remain shrouded in mystery, which was just the way Paige liked it. He was supposedly born on July 7, 1906, in Mobile, Alabama, but some people put his real birth year around 1900. His given name was Leroy, but when he lugged suitcases for train passengers back and forth, he was dubbed "Satchel."

Like Babe Ruth, Paige learned his baseball skills, and especially his pitching skills, as a teenager in reform school. He began his career in the Negro Leagues in 1927 with the Birmingham Black Barons. Over the next twenty years, he played for a half dozen other clubs, as well as participated

in hundreds of games on barnstorming tours.

Paige was a great pitcher, and he was enormously popular, drawing huge crowds. He had two fastballs: "Long Tommy" was his fastest, while "Little Tommy" was a notch below. He also had his "bee ball," so-called because it "would be where I want it to be."

A born self-promoter, Paige was often so unhittable that he would advertise that he would strike out the first nine men in the batting order—and then do it. He frequently pitched against teams of white all-stars and humbled them. Joe DiMaggio called him the best pitcher he had ever faced.

Because of the variations in the recording of Negro League statistics, no one knows precisely how many lifetime games he won. Some estimates put the number at about 2,000 games, in more than 2,500 starts. Inevitably, pitching that much and throwing so hard gave Paige arm trouble. Later in his career, he developed several "hesitation" pitches and deliveries that baffled batters and made him an even better pitcher.

In 1948, after baseball's racial barrier had been broken, Paige signed with the Cleveland Indians in the American League. Already in his forties, he still compiled a 6–1 record that year with two shutouts and a 2.48 earned run average (ERA). During the 1950s, he pitched for the St. Louis Browns and amazingly made one final appearance in the majors in 1965 for the Kansas City Athletics, pitching three scoreless innings at the age of fifty-nine. He was inducted into the Hall of Fame in 1971.

Born in San Francisco just a few months after the earthquake of 1906, **JOE CRONIN** shook up many American League pitchers as one of the best-hitting shortstops in baseball history.

Cronin began his baseball career with the Pittsburgh Pirates in 1925, and after one good season at their minor league affiliate in Johnstown, Pennsylvania, he was promoted to the majors for the 1926 season. Once with the Pirates, though, Cronin played in very few games over the next two seasons, appearing mostly as a pinch hitter.

The Pirates gave up on him in 1928, and the American League Washington Senators purchased his contract. After a decent season in 1929, Cronin exploded with a great season in 1930. He batted .346, scored 127 runs, and had 126 RBIs.

After hitting over .300 and driving in more than 115 runs in each of the next two years, Cronin was named player-manager for the Senators in 1933. While player-managers were common in Cronin's era, his selection was met with great surprise because he was just twenty-six years old. Cronin quickly quieted the doubters when he led the Senators to the pennant that same year. Unfortunately, Washington lost to the New York Giants in the World Series.

The Senators fell to seventh place the following year and lost money, so they sold Cronin's contract to the Boston Red Sox for a staggering sum of $250,000—the highest amount ever paid for a baseball player's contract at the time.

Again serving as player-manager, Cronin proved that he was worth the money by hitting over .300 six times in eleven years for the Red Sox, with his high of .325 coming in 1938. Despite his efforts, he failed to bring the pennant to Boston. It was only after Cronin broke his leg in 1945 and retired as an active player to manage full-time that he led the Red Sox to success in 1946. They lost the World Series that year to the St. Louis Cardinals.

Cronin finished his career with a .301 lifetime batting average, 170 home runs, and eight years with 100 or more RBIs. His power numbers were quite impressive, coming from a position that was traditionally thought to be a light-hitting one. He was considered the finest shortstop in baseball during the 1930s and the early 1940s.

Cronin remained active in baseball after his career ended, and in 1959, he was appointed president of the American League—the first former player to take up that office. He held the position for fourteen years. Cronin was inducted into the Hall of Fame in 1956.

Nicknamed "The Beast," both for his physique and his extraordinary power, **JIMMIE FOXX** terrorized American League pitchers for seventeen years, setting numerous hitting records along the way.

Born on a farm in Sudlersville, Maryland, in 1907, James Emory Foxx was a star high school athlete in both baseball and track, who had developed incredible strength lifting hay bales and working in the fields. Frank "Home Run" Baker was managing the Easton, Maryland, team when he heard about the muscular kid. He scouted Foxx, liked what he saw, and in no time, Foxx was playing for Baker, who put him behind the plate. Baker had been a star on Connie Mack's great pennant-winning Philadelphia A's teams from 1910 to 1914, and in 1924, Baker steered Foxx to the A's as a favor to Mack.

For the first three years, Foxx hardly played because the A's already had baseball's best catcher, Mickey Cochrane.

However, by 1929, Foxx was ready to play every day. Along with such players as Al Simmons and Lefty Grove, he became the heart of Mack's last great team, which won three straight pennants from 1929 to 1931 and two World Series. Foxx, who had settled in at first base after stints at third and catcher, hit 100 homers during those three years. He also batted .344 in eighteen World Series games.

As good as Foxx was in those years, he was simply sensational in 1932. He hit .364 with 58 homers and 169 RBIs and won the Most Valuable Player (MVP) Award. Foxx even topped himself the next year when he led the league with .356 in hitting, 48 home runs, and 163 RBIs, winning the Triple Crown as well as another MVP Award. Foxx surpassed .330 in the next two seasons with 80 more home runs, but despite his continued great success, his time in Philadelphia was coming to an end. After the 1935 season, Mack sold the contracts for Foxx and three other players to the Boston Red Sox for $300,000 due to financial difficulties. This was the last move in the dismantling of his team that had begun in 1933.

Foxx thrived in Boston. His first year there, he hit .338, with 41 homers and 143 RBIs. In 1938, he slammed 50 homers with 175 RBIs, and won an unprecedented third MVP Award. And his ferocious hitting left a lasting impression.

"I never saw anyone hit a baseball harder," said teammate Ted Williams.

Foxx retired after the 1945 season. He ended his career with 534 home runs, second at that time only to Babe Ruth, a .325 average, and 1,921 RBIs. He was elected to the Hall of Fame in 1951.

Possibly the slowest man in baseball history, **ERNIE LOMBARDI**'s lack of speed makes his .306 lifetime batting average that much more impressive, especially because the big catcher certainly never beat out any infield hits.

Lombardi was born in Oakland, California, the son of a small grocery store owner. As a young man, he drove a delivery truck for his father's business and played semipro ball when he had the chance. The local minor league club, the Oakland Oaks, tried to sign him, but Lombardi turned them down because he didn't want to leave home. However, Lombardi eventually got tired of working in the family business and changed his mind. Oakland was still interested and signed him in 1926.

Lombardi broke into the majors with the Brooklyn Dodgers, who bought his contract for $50,000, just in time for the 1931 season. However, the Dodgers had another young, solid catcher at the time, so they decided to trade Lombardi to the Cincinnati Reds prior to the 1932 season. Lombardi immediately became the team's number one catcher and a hitting star.

In ten seasons with the Reds, Lombardi hit over .300 seven times. In 1938, he hit .342 and won both the National League batting title and the league's Most Valuable Player (MVP) Award. That year, he also caught both of Johnny Vander Meer's back-to-back no-hitters.

Despite his large size—he was six foot three and 230 pounds—Lombardi was an excellent defensive catcher with a very strong throwing arm. He often threw out runners trying to steal second base without getting up from his crouch.

Lombardi was also incredibly slow afoot, and infielders frequently played back on the outfield grass for him, so that they could field his hot smashes and still throw him out. His lack of speed was so legendary that, once he stole second base without a throw in a game against Brooklyn. The Dodger infielders were so stunned that he was running that they didn't bother covering second base.

In 1939, Lombardi helped the Reds win their first pennant in twenty years, but they lost the World Series to the New York Yankees. The next year, Lombardi hit .319 as the Reds won the pennant again, and this time, they won the world championship, beating the Detroit Tigers in seven games.

In 1942, the Reds traded Lombardi to the Boston Braves, and he responded by winning his second batting title with a .330 average. After the season, he moved to the New York Giants, where he finished up his career in 1947. Lombardi retired with a .306 lifetime batting average and was voted into the Hall of Fame in 1986.

LEFTY GOMEZ was known as "Goofy" for his self-deprecating wit and one-liners, but he did not make opposing American League batters laugh very much in the 1930s as he continually got them out with his fastball and dazzling curve.

Vernon Louis Gomez was born in Rodeo, California, in 1908. As a young man, the tall, slim pitcher was a fireballer. After playing in the minor leagues for the San Francisco Seals, Gomez went up to the majors with the New York Yankees in 1930. Pitching in 15 games that season, Gomez was hardly impressive, with a 2–5 record.

The next year, though, was a completely different story. As a regular starter, he was 21–9 with 150 strikeouts and a 2.63 earned run average (ERA). He followed that with a 24–7 record in 1932, and then, after falling off to 16 wins in 1933, he had his career year in 1934, when he led the American League in four pitching categories: 26 wins, 2.33 ERA, 158 strikeouts, and 6 shutouts.

Gomez quickly became one of the most popular teammates on the Yankees. When he was asked to what he owed his pitching success, he replied, "Clean living and a fast outfield." Gomez was afflicted with various arm ailments throughout his career, and as time went on, he became more of a pitcher who relied more on control rather than speed. "I'm throwing as hard as I ever did, but the ball is just not getting there as fast," Gomez cracked.

Nevertheless, the ball got there fast enough for Gomez to lead the American League in strikeouts three times and in wins and ERA twice. Overall, he won 189 games in his fourteen-year career.

Gomez was also at his best in big games. He was the winning pitcher in three All-Star games during the 1930s and was the Yankees' ace southpaw pitcher on their great run of four straight world championships, from 1936 to 1939. Including his appearance in the 1932 Fall Classic, Gomez was undefeated in the five World Series he played in, with a 6–0 record and an excellent 2.86 ERA. His six victories without a single loss are a World Series record.

Gomez could find humor in any situation. One time, catcher Bill Dickey came out to the mound to ask Gomez what he wanted to throw to the massive and muscular Jimmie Foxx, who was waiting at the plate.

"I don't want to throw him nothing," responded Gomez. "Maybe he'll get tired of waiting and leave."

Gomez retired in 1943, and later had a second career as a speaker and guest on radio shows. In 1972, he was elected to the Hall of Fame.

Possibly the nicest guy who ever played the game of baseball, **MEL OTT** was a deadly hitter with an unusual batting style that earned him more than 500 lifetime home runs.

Born in Gretna, Louisiana, in 1909, Ott was small when he was young, but he still starred in baseball, football, and basketball in high school. After being rejected by a minor league team because of his size, Ott joined a semipro team managed by New York Giants manager John McGraw's (see no. 4) scouts. The scout saw Ott hit and tipped off McGraw, who brought Ott to New York for a tryout.

The left-handed hitting youngster proceeded to smash one batting practice pitch after another into the right field stands. McGraw decided right then and there to sign him, despite the fact that he was only sixteen years old.

Ott had a highly unusual batting style. He would lift his front foot into the air before swinging, as if he was stepping over something in front of him. McGraw was afraid that if he sent him down to the minors, somebody would alter his style and ruin him. To prevent that, McGraw kept Ott on the big league roster and played him only sparingly in the outfield during his first few years. Ott sat near McGraw on the bench, and the veteran manager taught him the finer points of the game. As a result, Ott acquired a nickname of "Master Melvin."

By 1928, Ott was ready to become a regular. He hit .322 with 18 homers that year, and followed that up with a .328 average, 42 homers, and 152 RBIs the next year. He was the classic home field slugger, with a style perfectly suited for the short right field wall at the Giants' Polo Grounds, 257 feet from home plate. Of his 511 lifetime home runs, only 187 were hit on the road.

Still, as an overall hitter, Ott was a terror. He led or tied for the lead in the National League in home runs six times. While he never won a batting title, he hit better than .300 ten times in his career and retired with a lifetime average of .304. He helped lead the Giants to three pennants and one world championship during the 1930s.

Ott spent his entire twenty-two-year career with the Giants, and in 1942, he became the team's player-manager. With Ott as manager, the Giants never finished higher than third over the next six seasons. He retired as a player in 1947 and was replaced as manager the next season. He was inducted into the Hall of Fame in 1951.

◆ **DIZZY DEAN** blazed through the baseball sky for only a few short years, but while he did, there wasn't a better right-handed pitcher in the game—or a more colorful character.

He was born Jay Hanna Dean in Lucas, Arkansas, the son of an itinerant farm worker. As a young man, Dean joined the U.S. Army, where he learned to pitch and acquired his nickname of "Dizzy."

After being discharged, Dean was discovered by St. Louis Cardinals scouts while playing sandlot ball. He signed with St. Louis and went up to the majors in 1932.

Dean quickly became a central figure in the famous Gashouse Gang, the name given to the Cardinals of the early 1930s because it contained so many wacky characters. Dizzy enjoyed playing the part of the uneducated hick, keeping his teammates, reporters, and the public amused with his antics and poor English.

The country bumpkin façade masked an intelligent man and a fine pitcher. "It ain't bragging if you go out and do it," he said, and from 1932 to 1936, Dean did it. He averaged 24 victories per year and led the league in strikeouts and complete games four times. In 1934, he won 30 games to win the National League's Most Valuable Player (MVP) Award. He was the last National League pitcher in the twentieth century to win 30 games in a season.

In the Cardinals' victorious 1934 World Series against the Detroit Tigers, Dean won two games. His teammate, who was his brother Paul, won the other two. Dean gained almost as much notoriety in the Series by getting beaned in the fourth game. Brought unconscious to the hospital, Dean later announced, "They X-rayed my head and found nothing."

Dean was confident and cocky on the mound, bearing down when the game was close, but virtually calling out what pitch he was going to throw during a rout. "Son, what kind of a pitch would you like to miss?" he sometimes asked opposing batters.

During the 1937 All-Star Game, a batter's line drive broke Dean's toe. He tried coming back too soon after the injury, altered his pitching motion, and hurt his arm.

He was never the same pitcher again. He retired in 1940 at the age of thirty with 150 lifetime victories in just ten seasons.

After his retirement, Dizzy enjoyed a second career as a television baseball broadcaster, while cheerfully mangling English grammar to the dismay of teachers around the country. However, he continued to be wildly popular with fans everywhere. He was elected to the Hall of Fame in 1953.

Of all the Black ballplayers who were barred from the major leagues because of the color line, **JOSH GIBSON** was perhaps the most tragic victim.

Gibson was the son of a sharecropper from Buena Vista, Georgia. When he was a boy, his father moved the entire family to Pittsburgh, Pennsylvania, and went to work in the steel mills. As a teenager, Gibson began playing semipro baseball as a catcher, although he had planned on becoming an electrician.

One night, he was watching a Negro League game featuring the Homestead Grays when their only catcher became unavailable. Desperate, the Grays saw Gibson sitting in the stands and called on him to catch. From then on, he no longer thought much about the electrical trade.

Before long, Gibson was a genuine star of Black baseball. In 1934, he jumped from the Grays to their rival team, the Pittsburgh Crawfords. There he teamed up with ace pitcher Satchel Paige to make the Crawfords

virtually invincible, and for the next few years they ruled Black baseball.

According to most observers, Gibson was a prodigious slugger who had no equal—not even Babe Ruth. However, due to the extreme variations and difficulties facing Black baseball in terms of record keeping, there is no way to know exactly what Gibson's real statistical totals were. However, it's believed that he hit at least 70 homers in several seasons, when Ruth's 60 remained the standard for major league baseball. Over his lifetime, Gibson's home run total is thought to be around 800.

Gibson's strength and power were legendary. In his exhibition games against white major leaguers—the only time that he got to measure his skills against big leaguers—he put on some awesome demonstrations in various major league ballparks. He is reputed to have hit the longest home runs in several stadiums, including the Forbes Field in Pittsburgh and the Crosley Field in Cincinnati. One of the reasons Gibson's skills were so admired is because of how well he did in these exhibitions. In 16 games against some of the finest talent in the pro ranks, Gibson hit .424 with four homers.

Gibson returned to the Homestead Grays in 1937, and except for two years in the Mexican League, he played for them for the rest of his career. Frustrated at being barred from the majors, Gibson began drinking heavily in the early 1940s, and his skills began to decline dramatically.

By 1946, when Jackie Robinson signed with the Brooklyn Dodgers and was assigned to their Montreal farm team, Gibson's career was over. He died of a stroke in 1947—just three months before Robinson made his major league debut with the Dodgers. Gibson was elected to the Hall of Fame in 1972.

◆ A great slugger whose career was seriously shortened by service in World War II, **HANK GREENBERG** was one of the American League's most dominant hitters during the 1930s.

Born and raised in New York City, Greenberg was an excellent high school athlete who attracted the attention of major league baseball scouts. The Detroit Tigers made Greenberg a very appealing offer: they would pay for Greenberg's education and delay his career until after he had gone to college. Greenberg accepted the offer.

However, after one semester in college, Greenberg decided he wanted to try baseball full-time. He spent a few years in the minors, and then became the regular Detroit first baseman in 1933, hitting .301 that year. The following season, he led the Tigers to the first of their four American League pennants during his career, hitting .339 with 26 homers, 163 RBIs, and a league-leading 63 doubles.

In 1935, Greenberg hit .328, led the league with 36 homers, had 170 RBIs, and was named the American League's Most Valuable Player (MVP). The Tigers won the pennant and their first world championship, beating the Chicago Cubs in the World Series.

After missing much of the 1936 season due to a broken wrist, Greenberg put up great home run and RBI totals for the next four seasons. During that time, he averaged 43 homers and 147 RBIs a season.

In 1940, Greenberg moved to left field so that the Tigers could get another slugging first baseman, Rudy York, into their lineup. He made the transition gracefully, and at the plate, he had another great year, winning his second MVP Award as the Tigers won the pennant again.

Like many other players of the era, Greenberg lost much time serving in the armed forces during World War II. He enlisted in 1941 and didn't rejoin the team until midway through the 1945 season. He hit a dramatic grand slam against the St. Louis Browns in the final game to win the pennant for the Tigers. He then led them to another world championship, hitting .304, with two home runs and seven RBIs in their victory over the Chicago Cubs.

After a salary dispute, Greenberg was traded to the Pittsburgh Pirates in 1946., but he retired after playing just one more year.

Throughout his career, Greenberg carried an additional burden as the first high-profile Jewish superstar ballplayer. He often endured terrible verbal abuse and mindless prejudice, but to his credit, he ignored it and continued to perform superbly on the field. After his retirement, Greenberg was a baseball executive for several teams. He was inducted into the Hall of Fame in 1956.

Whether it was hitting a home run, making a defensive play, or sliding into a base, **JOE DIMAGGIO** personified grace and style on a baseball field.

Although he was born in Martinez, California, DiMaggio will forever be associated with San Francisco. He grew up in the city by the Bay Area and played sandlot baseball there along with his two brothers, Vince and Dom. Vince had played with the minor league San Francisco Seals, and in 1932, Joe signed with them as well.

The following year, DiMaggio had major league scouts across America panting with anticipation when he hit in 61 straight games with a .340 batting average. The next year, he hit .341 but suffered a knee injury that caused many major league clubs to lose interest in him. However, the New York Yankees remained interested and signed him for the bargain basement price of $25,000 in 1934.

DiMaggio went up to the Yankees in 1936 when they were a team in transition. Babe Ruth had left after the 1934 season, and Lou Gehrig had taken over as the club's leader. The team had only won one pennant during the 1930s, in 1932. DiMaggio contributed with an outstanding rookie year, and the team began a new era of dominance. He hit .323 with 29 homers and 125 RBIs to help the Yankees win the first of an unprecedented four consecutive World Series titles.

DiMaggio had an even greater season in 1937, hitting .346 and leading the league with 46 home runs and 151 RBIs. In 1939, when Gehrig was stricken with the fatal illness that would claim his life, DiMaggio became the team leader. In 1941, he set a record that many baseball experts feel will never be broken, hitting in 56 straight games.

Above all, DiMaggio was a winner. The Yankees won ten pennants and nine world championships in his thirteen seasons. He displayed his competitive fire in 1949, when he returned to the lineup in mid-June after missing two months due to a heel injury. He hit four homers against the Boston Red Sox in three games, and he hit .346 for the rest of the season. The Yankees won the pennant over Boston by one game that year.

With a lifetime average of .325, DiMaggio was a contact hitter who rarely struck out. He had 361 lifetime homers and struck out just 369 times. He was also a superlative outfielder with great instincts, who could make every catch look easy as he roamed far and wide in Yankee Stadium's cavernous center field.

DiMaggio retired after the 1951 season and was inducted into the Hall of Fame in 1955.

Small in stature, when **PHIL RIZZUTO** stepped onto a baseball field, he cast a giant shadow as shortstop on the great Yankee teams of the 1940s and 1950s.

Philip Francis Rizzuto was born in New York City in 1917. Only five foot six and 150 pounds soaking wet, he had to struggle all his life against misconceptions that his size made him unfit for the job. In 1936, having played high school ball, he tried out for the Brooklyn Dodgers. Manager Casey Stengel sent him home because he thought Rizzuto was too small, saying, "Get a shoebox, kid. You can't play."

Undaunted, Rizzuto showed up at a Yankees tryout the following year. He was given a ham sandwich, a glass of milk, and a chance to demonstrate his abilities. Impressed, the Yankees signed him to a minor league contract. His father pinned a $20 bill to his undershirt and wished him good luck.

Rizzuto had more than luck on his

side—he had skill. After winning the Minor League Player of the Year Award, he went up to the Yankees in 1941. Shunned by the team's veterans at first, he was befriended by Joe DiMaggio, and Rizzuto rewarded the superstar's faith by hitting .307 in his rookie season.

Rizzuto was one of the best bunters in baseball. One year, during a game late in the season, the Yankees and the Boston Red Sox were battling it out for the pennant. With the game hanging in the balance, and DiMaggio streaking for home from third on a suicide squeeze, Rizzuto laid down a perfect bunt to bring him in for the game's only run. He led the American League in sacrifice hits for four straight years, from 1949 to 1952. No one had ever done that before.

In 1950, Rizzuto had his best year, hitting .324 with 36 doubles, while winning the league's Most Valuable Player (MVP) Award. Nicknamed "Scooter" by his teammates, Rizzuto played on Yankee teams that won ten pennants and eight world championships.

In the field, Rizzuto was quick and sure, making all the plays, both routine and otherwise. "He's the greatest shortstop I have ever seen," said the same Casey Stengel—now his Yankee manager—who had once dismissed him for being too small. Yankee pitcher Vic Raschi said that his best pitch was "anything the batter grounds, lines, or pops in the direction of Rizzuto."

After he retired in 1956, he began a new career as a broadcaster, rooting as fervently for the Yankees behind the microphone as he had done on the field. Rizzuto was elected to the Hall of Fame in 1994.

PEE WEE REESE was the glue that held the great infielders of the Brooklyn Dodgers together during the 1940s and 1950s. More importantly, he befriended Jackie Robinson in 1947, which helped pave the way for the monumental Black player's acceptance in the team as well as in all of major league baseball.

Born in Ekron, Kentucky, Harold Henry Reese acquired his nickname from the marble he used to win a championship at age twelve. He was a good high school and semipro player and was signed by the Louisville Colonels of the minor league American Association in 1938. After Reese had two fine seasons with Louisville, the Brooklyn Dodgers bought his contract for $75,000.

Reese joined the Dodgers in 1940, and immediately proved to be a stabilizing influence on the team, especially in the infield. The following year, Brooklyn won its first pennant in twenty years. The Dodgers lost to the New York Yankees in the World Series that year, beginning one of baseball's most storied rivalries.

A measure of Reese's worth to the Dodgers is shown by the fact that while he was in the navy during World War II, the team never finished better than third. Once he returned in 1946, the team won six National League flags over eleven years and one World Series in 1955.

Never a great hitter, Reese batted over .300 just once with the Dodgers—.309 in 1954. However, Reese was such a superb fielder, excellent bat handler, and steadying influence on pitchers that the Dodgers simply couldn't win without him. He was the team's captain and was also called "The Little Colonel" because of his Kentucky background.

Perhaps Reese never demonstrated his leadership skills to a greater degree than when Jackie Robinson joined the Dodgers in 1947 as the first Black player in the majors. Reese had initially requested a trade from the Dodgers when they obtained Robinson, but he soon thought better of it.

The pressure on Robinson was enormous. During a game early in the season, Reese walked over to Robinson and put his arm around his shoulders. The message was clear: Robinson and Reese were friends and teammates. Through gestures such as that and other actions, Reese made it more than obvious that he had accepted Robinson and that others should do the same. It united the Dodgers behind Robinson, which helped him weather the insults and taunts from racist spectators and opposing players.

As almost any Brooklyn fan in the 1940s and 1950s would agree, Pee Wee Reese was the heart and soul of those great Dodger teams. He was elected to the Hall of Fame in 1984.

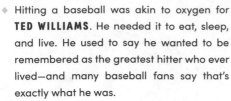

Hitting a baseball was akin to oxygen for **TED WILLIAMS**. He needed it to eat, sleep, and live. He used to say he wanted to be remembered as the greatest hitter who ever lived—and many baseball fans say that's exactly what he was.

Williams was born and raised in San Diego, California, and when he was just 17, he began his career with the San Diego Padres, a minor league franchise at the time. When he was nineteen, despite having just two years of professional experience, Williams was signed by the Boston Red Sox of the American League.

In 1938, Williams won the American Association's Triple Crown, with a .366 average, 43 homers, and 142 RBIs. He was ready to play in the majors—and although the Red Sox already had three good hitting outfielders, they made room for him.

In 1939, Williams made an immediate splash as a rookie when he hit .327 with 31 homers and a league-leading 145 RBIs. Two

years later, in 1941, Williams hit .406—the last man to hit over .400 in the twentieth century. The next season, Williams won his first Triple Crown, leading the league in averages, homers, and RBIs.

In 1943, Williams's career was interrupted for three years as he entered military service, and we can only imagine what his lifetime statistics would have been if he hadn't lost that time in the prime of his career. He later lost two more years to military service during the Korean War.

When he returned in 1946, Williams hit .342, won the first of two Most Valuable Player (MVP) Awards, and led the Red Sox to their only World Series appearance during his career. However, he hit only .200 in the Series as St. Louis beat Boston.

While baseball insiders readily acknowledged Williams's great talent, he was never a huge fan favorite. Early in his career, he developed an antagonistic relationship with the Boston press and Red Sox fans. While he was a great hitter, he appeared to merely tolerate other facets of the game, such as fielding. He also remained brash and outspoken, and refused to tip his cap to acknowledge the cheers of fans.

Williams retired after the 1960 season with some incredible lifetime numbers. He hit .344, won 6 batting titles, had 521 home runs, and had the highest on-base average of .483 in history. He was elected to the Hall of Fame in 1966. When he died, just two years before the Red Sox won the 2004 World Series, many obituaries granted him his wish of being called the greatest hitter in baseball history.

◆ **BOB FELLER** came roaring out of the cornfields of Van Meter, Iowa, as a fireballing teenager with a blazing fastball that had baseball analysts comparing him to the fastest pitcher of all time: Walter Johnson.

With strong encouragement from his father, young Feller was playing baseball from the time he was ten. At thirteen years old, he was competing against much older players, and at sixteen, the Cleveland Indians signed him to a contract, even though he was still in high school. The signing was invalid according to the rules then, but Commissioner Kenesaw Mountain Landis let the Indians keep Feller anyway, fearing a massive bidding war if he was declared a free agent.

When he was seventeen, Feller made his debut in an exhibition game against the St. Louis Cardinals. He was extremely fast but extremely wild, and the Cardinals player-manager Frankie Frisch took one look at him warming up and took himself out of the lineup. Feller struck out eight Cardinals in three innings that day.

He joined the Indians in 1936, appearing in fourteen games; he had a 5–3 record, and in one game struck out a record-tying seventeen batters. He then returned home to finish high school.

Feller continued to work on his control, and after fighting some arm trouble in 1937, he came into prominence the next season, when he won 17 games and fanned 240 batters. For the next three seasons, he led the American League in wins with 24, 27, and 25 games, and in strikeouts, with 246, 261, and 260. He also pitched the first Opening Day no-hitter in baseball history in 1940 against the Chicago White Sox.

No one knows what "Rapid Robert" would have accomplished if he had not gone into the navy right before the 1942 season.

He was just twenty-four years old and, arguably, entering his prime as a power pitcher. Feller returned to full-time action in 1946 and showed that the hiatus had not diminished his pitching skills. He won 26 games, struck out an amazing 348 batters, and also led the league in complete games with 36, and shutouts with 10.

Feller remained one of the league's top pitchers into the early 1950s. The Indians won two pennants during his career—in 1948 and 1954—and the world championship in 1948.

Feller retired after the 1956 season with 266 career victories and 2,581 strikeouts. He also pitched three no hitters and twelve one-hitters during his career, and he led the American League in strikeouts seven times. He was elected to the Hall of Fame in 1962.

No one ever came to the big leagues with more pressure on his shoulders than **JACKIE ROBINSON**. As the first Black player in major league baseball, he not only had to perform skillfully on the field but also endure bigotry and hostility from many spectators and opposing players—all the while adhering to a promise he had made to ignore the insults and not retaliate.

All of America was watching to see how he acted. Yet the true measure of Robinson's greatness is that, both on and off the field, he passed every test with flying colors.

Jack Roosevelt Robinson was born in Georgia, but it was in Pasadena, California, that he grew up and made a name for himself as a multisport star at the junior college there. He then attended the University of California, Los Angeles (UCLA), where he lettered in baseball, basketball, football, and track.

After serving in the army as a lieutenant in World War II, Robinson signed with the

Kansas City Monarchs of the Negro League in 1945. At that time, Branch Rickey of the Brooklyn Dodgers came to him with an offer to break baseball's color line.

While other teams had made half-hearted offers in the past to bring a Black player into the major leagues, Rickey's offer was serious. Robinson signed with Brooklyn, and after a brilliant season in the minors, he went up to the Dodgers in 1947.

In his first season, Robinson hit .297, led the league with 29 stolen bases, and was named Rookie of the Year. Thereafter, Robinson hit over .300 nearly every year, winning the National League batting title with a .342 average in 1949. After starting out as a first baseman with Brooklyn, he switched to second and remained there for most of his career.

Robinson was also one of the most exciting base runners of all time, and his steals home electrified crowds. He brought the running, wide-open style of Negro League baseball to the majors and re-energized the sport. Robinson was perhaps the key component of the Dodger team that won six pennants and one World Series from 1947 to 1956. Many attribute that winning streak to his ability and competitive fire.

Although Robinson did not have a lengthy major league career and played for just ten years, he managed a lifetime .311 average. More importantly, his presence off the field changed major league baseball forever, opening the door not only to hundreds of other Black players but also to Hispanic players later on.

After he retired, Robinson remained an untiring advocate of equal rights for Black Americans in all areas of baseball, particularly in the administrative and managerial areas. He was elected to the Hall of Fame in 1962.

If it was not for an injury that presumably destroyed his initial career, **STAN MUSIAL** may never have realized his full potential as one of the greatest hitters of all time.

Born in Donora, Pennsylvania, in 1920, Stanley Frank Musial was a triple threat in high school as a star first baseman, an outfielder, and an outstanding pitcher. After he signed with the St. Louis Cardinals in 1938, he was assigned to the Daytona Beach Islanders in the Florida State League, where he played outfield on days he did not pitch. His manager was former big league pitcher Dickie Kerr.

One day during the 1940 season, Musial was in the outfield when he tried to make a play and landed heavily on his left (pitching) shoulder, injuring it so badly that his career on the mound was over. A distraught Musial was ready to quit baseball, but then Kerr said something so wise that it changed the course of Musial's life.

"Let's stay with it," said Kerr. "I think you can become a pretty good outfielder. You're already a pretty good hitter."

Truer words had never been spoken. Musial switched to the outfield full-time and became a terrific hitter. In two minor league stops, he hit .379 and .326. When he was promoted to the Cardinals at the tail end of the 1941 season, Musial hit .426 in a dozen games. He never went back to the minors.

When Musial joined St. Louis, they were on the verge of blossoming into a National League powerhouse, and Musial was the last piece of the pennant-winning puzzle. From 1942 to 1946, the Cardinals won four pennants and three world championships. Musial's averages during these pennant-winning years were .315, .357, .347, and .365. He won the Most Valuable Player (MVP) Award in 1943 and again in1946, and in both years, he led the league in hitting, slugging percentages, hits, doubles, and triples.

The left-handed Musial had one of the most unique batting styles in baseball. He would twist himself into a knot until he resembled a human corkscrew. When he uncoiled, his bat would whip around with terrific speed.

Musial won his third MVP Award in 1948, when he hit .376, with an astounding .702 slugging average, and led the league again in hits, doubles, and triples.

Musial spent his entire career with the Cardinals and was one of the most popular players in the history of the franchise. He retired after the 1963 season, with 7 batting titles, 475 home runs, and 1,951 RBIs. A lifetime .331 hitter, he was elected to the Hall of Fame in 1969.

Major league baseball's first Black catcher, **ROY CAMPANELLA**, had a brilliant career that was tragically ended by an automobile accident that left him paralyzed for life.

The Philadelphia-born son of a Black mother and a white father, Campanella was so good of a player, that at age fifteen, he quit school and began catching for the semipro Bacharach Giants. In 1937, he moved on to the Baltimore Elite Giants of the Negro Leagues, and soon after that, he was catching star pitchers like Satchel Paige.

The ban on Black ballplayers kept Campanella in the Negro Leagues up through the mid-1940s. When Branch Rickey of the Dodgers was looking for players to break baseball's color line, Campanella made his short list. In 1945, Rickey first signed Jackie Robinson (see no. 48), and then in 1946, he signed Campanella.

After two seasons being named Most Valuable Player (MVP) in both of the minor leagues in which he played, Campanella went up to the Dodgers in 1948, the year after Robinson made baseball history. By 1949, Campanella was firmly established as the team's number one catcher.

The Brooklyn Dodgers were on the verge of becoming the dominant team in the National League, and Campanella played a big part in that. A sensational defensive player and a tremendous hitter, "Campy" also had the ability to get the best out of the Dodger pitching staff. The result was a team that won five pennants and one World Series title from 1949 to 1956.

Campanella's heavy hitting was an integral part of the Dodgers' offensive attack. During the 1950s, he won three National League MVP Awards in 1951, 1953, and 1955. From 1949 to 1955, he averaged nearly 30 home runs and 100 RBIs each year.

As one of the first Black players to integrate baseball, Campanella suffered frequent verbal abuse. However, Campy was a genial man, and he never lost his enthusiasm for playing. "You got to be a man to play baseball for a living, but you got to have a lot of little boy in you too," Campanella often said.

In 1958, Campanella was preparing to head west with the Dodgers as they moved to their new home in Los Angeles. However, in January that year, he had an automobile accident that left him paralyzed, suddenly ending his career.

Despite the tragedy, Campanella never lost his optimistic outlook on life. After his recovery from the accident, he later served as a spring training coach for the Dodgers for many years. He also wrote an inspirational autobiography, *It's Good to Be Alive*, that was later turned into a televised movie. He was inducted into the Hall of Fame in 1969.

A late-blooming success who didn't win his first game until he was twenty-five years old, **WARREN SPAHN** finished his career as the winningest left-handed pitcher in baseball history.

Born in Buffalo, New York, to a baseball-loving father, Spahn started out as a first baseman. However, he switched to the mound when he found out that he couldn't hit well enough to make the grade as a position player.

The Boston Braves signed him in 1940. He spent most of the next three seasons in the minors, although he was briefly with the parent club in 1942. He then enlisted in the army during World War II.

When he returned from the service, Spahn became a reliever and part-time starter with the Braves in 1946, going 8–5. He blossomed into a star the following year, with a 21–10 record and a league-leading 2.33 earned run average (ERA).

In 1948, Spahn teamed up with Johnny Sain as the Braves' one-two pitching punch to lead the team to a surprising National League pennant. With few other reliable pitchers in the rotation, the burden for winning important games fell on the duo. Braves fans even took up a familiar refrain that year: "It's Spahn and Sain and pray for rain."

The following year, Spahn won 21 games to lead the National League. He repeated the feat in 1950. Altogether, Spahn won more than 20 games thirteen times and led the National League in victories eight times. In 1957, he won the league's Cy Young Award with a 21–11 mark and a 2.69 ERA.

When the Braves moved to Milwaukee in 1953 and became a powerhouse team in the late 1950s, winning two pennants in 1957 and 1958 and one world championship in 1957, Spahn became a vital cog in their machine. Although he didn't have a blazing fastball, he featured a variety of pitches and used pinpoint control to baffle hitters.

In an era in which most ballplayers did not play past thirty-five years old, Spahn was still an effective big league pitcher well into his forties. In 1963, he hooked up with Giants' future Hall-of-Famer Juan Marichal (see no. 74) in one of the most memorable pitching duels of the decade. Both hurlers threw matching shutouts for 15 innings until Willie Mays hit a home run off Spahn in the sixteenth to win the game 1–0. While Marichal was only twenty-five years old at the time, Spahn had just turned forty-two. Remarkably, Spahn went on to win 23 games that year.

Spahn retired after the 1965 season with 363 wins. In 1973, he was inducted into the Hall of Fame.

RALPH KINER once said, "Singles hitters drive Fords. Home run hitters drive Cadillacs." After he burst upon the baseball scene in the late 1940s, Kiner became the National League's first player to earn $100,000 annually. Fittingly, he promptly bought himself a Cadillac.

Ralph Kiner was the epitome of the 1950s baseball slugger. A big man at six foot two and 195 pounds, he was neither swift nor particularly graceful in the outfield. What he could do well, though, was hit a baseball a long way—arguably better than anybody else of his generation.

Born in New Mexico, Kiner grew up in California and was a star high school and semipro baseball player. He received several offers from various clubs to begin his pro career in the low minor leagues, but the Pittsburgh Pirates of the National League offered to start him in the high minors, so he signed with them.

The Pirates made Kiner such an offer because, at the time, they were one of the worst teams in baseball and virtually devoid of all prospects. Kiner played a little more than two seasons in the minors, then went into military service. When he came out, he worked like a demon preparing for the upcoming 1946 season. His spring training performance was sensational, and he became the Pirates starting left fielder from there on out.

Kiner's 23 homers in 1946 led the league. It was the first of seven straight years in which he led or tied for the lead in home runs. In 1947, he belted 51 homers and followed that up in 1949 with 54 round-trippers—the most in his career. He also knocked in more than 100 runs for five straight seasons.

Kiner belted his blasts into a section of Pittsburgh's Forbes Field that fans came to call "Kiner's Korner." During the years that Kiner played with the Pirates, they usually finished near the bottom of the standings, and he was the club's only gate attraction.

However, the Pirates traded him to the Chicago Cubs in 1953 because of a contract dispute. Kiner played just two years with the Cubs before finishing out his career in 1955 with the Cleveland Indians. When he retired because of a chronic bad back, Kiner's home run ratio versus times at bat was second only to Babe Ruth's. He ended with 369 career home runs.

During his career, Kiner was also a prime mover in a movement that eventually led to the formation of the players' union. Later Kiner became a popular broadcaster with the New York Mets. He was inducted into the Hall of Fame in 1975.

◆ Baseball's first real relief specialist, **HOYT WILHELM** dazzled and confused hitters for more than twenty years with a pitch that he barely threw hard enough to break a pane of glass.

James Hoyt Wilhelm was a big baseball fan growing up in Huntersville, North Carolina. As a youngster, he used to listen to broadcasts for the Washington Senators, who had a pitcher named Emil "Dutch" Leonard who was a specialist with a pitch called the knuckleball. A 1939 newspaper article described how the pitch was thrown. Wilhelm studied it and practiced the pitch until he mastered it.

Wilhelm began his professional career in 1942, and after three years of military service, he continued to kick around the minors until 1952.

That year, Wilhelm burst onto the baseball scene as an unknown relief pitcher with the New York Giants. He had a sensational rookie season, winning 15 games, saving 11 more, and posting a league-leading 2.43 earned run average (ERA). It was the first time in major league history that a pitcher had won an ERA title without pitching a complete game. In 1954, Wilhelm had a league-best 12 relief wins as he helped the Giants win the pennant and then upset the favored Cleveland Indians in the World Series.

After a subpar 1956 season, Wilhelm was traded to the St. Louis Cardinals in 1957, beginning an odyssey that would see him pitch for nine teams in his major league career. By 1958, he was pitching for the Cleveland Indians when he made his first major league start. Later that season he was traded to the Baltimore Orioles, and on September 2, Wilhelm started a game against the Yankees and threw a no-hitter.

The next season, used almost exclusively as a starter, Wilhelm won 15 games and led the American League in ERA with a 2.19 mark, becoming the first pitcher ever to lead both leagues in ERA.

Following the 1960 season, Wilhelm again became a relief specialist exclusively. And the saves began to pile up, amounting to lifetime stats of 227 saves and 143 victories.

Although there had been other pitchers who had been used primarily as relievers in the past, Wilhelm was the first to carve out a successful, long-term career as a relief specialist. Because the knuckleball is easy on the arm, he was able to pitch until the age of forty-eight. Catchers used oversized gloves when he pitched because his knuckleball was so unpredictable that it would dart and dance across the plate. Even Wilhelm himself did not know for certain where the pitch was going once it left his hand.

He was inducted into the Hall of Fame in 1985.

LARRY DOBY was the second Black player signed to play major league baseball and the first in the American League.

Although he was born in Camden, South Carolina, Doby became one of New Jersey's top high school athletes, which is where Doby's family moved after his father died. While he attended Long Island University, Doby began playing baseball at age seventeen under an assumed name for the Newark Eagles of the Negro League.

Doby played for the Eagles from 1942 to 1946, minus the two years he served in the navy during World War II. In 1947, he was batting a sensational .414 in August when Bill Veeck, maverick owner of the Cleveland Indians, signed him.

The signing was a bittersweet experience for the Eagles. While they were happy to see Doby get his chance to play major league ball, the Eagles received little compensation for one of their rising stars. Signings such as this one helped hasten the demise of the Negro Leagues and Black baseball in general.

Doby played briefly with Cleveland during 1947, and the following year, he helped spark Cleveland's drive to the pennant. He hit .301 with 14 homers and 66 runs batted in. In the Indians' World Series triumph over the Boston Braves, Doby batted .318 and hit a home run that proved decisive in Cleveland's game four victory.

An infielder in the Negro Leagues, Doby moved to center field with the Indians and soon proved to be one of the best defensive outfielders in the league. As a hitter, he twice led the league in home runs—with 32 in both 1951 and 1954—and averaged nearly 100 RBIs over seven seasons.

Doby left the Indians after the 1955 season in a trade with the Chicago White Sox. Overall, he played for thirteen years, compiling a .283 lifetime batting average with 253 home runs.

As the second Black player in the majors, Doby was subjected to the same racial intolerance that Jackie Robinson faced. Doby's experiences, however, were much less publicized, mainly because the media had focused so much on Robinson in 1947 that some of what happened later seemed like old news. In addition, Doby, a far less volatile personality than Robinson, tried to keep a low profile.

In 1978, Doby was once again second in a historic movement. He became the manager of the Chicago White Sox, becoming the second Black manager at the major league level. He was inducted into the Hall of Fame in 1998.

Known far and wide for his humorous sayings and malapropisms, **YOGI BERRA** made people laugh for decades. Before that, he spent nineteen years giving American League pitchers nothing but grief as one of the best catchers and clutch hitters in baseball history.

Lawrence Peter Berra was born in St. Louis, Missouri, in 1925. As a kid, his friends called him "Lawdie" until one day, in a movie, they all saw a swami called a yoga. For no particular reason, "Lawdie" became "Yoga," which morphed over time into "Yogi."

When his boyhood pal Joe Garagiola received a $500 bonus to sign as a catcher with the St. Louis Cardinals, Berra wanted one too. However, the Cardinals apparently figured that one kid catcher was enough and refused to come up with the same money. The Yankees did, though, and signed him in 1943.

After brief stints in the minors and the U.S. Navy, Berra went up to the Yankees for good in 1947. He was a catcher and outfielder that season as the Yankees won another pennant and the World Series. However, Berra was embarrassed in the Series when the Dodgers stole several bases on him. He knew he had to improve his catching skills, so he worked endlessly with Yankees legend Bill Dickey. This led to the immortal Berra quote: "Bill Dickey learned me all his experiences."

That may have been the start of the "Yogiisms," the many sayings for which Berra became famous over the years, such as "When you get to a fork in the road, take it," or "It ain't over till it's over."

One thing that wasn't funny was Berra's hitting. A notorious "bad ball" hitter, he would slash at any pitch he liked, no matter how far out of the strike zone it fell. Although he never led the American League in any offensive category, he had 90 or more RBIs in nine seasons and socked 20 or more homers eleven times. He also won the league's Most Valuable Player (MVP) Award three times—in 1951, 1954, and 1955. Berra played in fourteen World Series during his nineteen-year career, which is more than anyone else in history. He also ranks first in World Series career hits and doubles and second in RBIs.

Once described by his manager Casey Stengel as "a peculiar fellow with amazing ability," Berra also shrewdly handled the vaunted Yankees pitching staff. "I am lucky to have him and so are my pitchers," said Stengel.

After he retired, Berra managed the Yankees and the Mets, winning pennants with both teams, but never the World Series. He was elected to the Hall of Fame in 1972.

A terrific hitter and fine center fielder, **DUKE SNIDER**'s career was somewhat overshadowed because he played the same position in the same town and at the same time as two of baseball's all-time greats: Mickey Mantle and Willie Mays. Nevertheless, in the 1950s, Snider put up some great offensive numbers and was a mainstay on the heralded Brooklyn Dodgers teams of that decade.

Edwin D. Snider was born in Los Angeles, California, and was a star athlete in high school. The Brooklyn Dodgers signed him right out of school, and Snider rewarded their faith in him by leading the Piedmont League in home runs.

Snider was a part-time player with the Dodgers in 1947 and 1948, but he struggled at the plate, striking out frequently. He was sent down to the minor leagues to better learn the strike zone, and when he returned to Brooklyn in 1949, he proved that the lessons had paid off by hitting .292 with 23 homers. The following year, Snider upped his homer total to 31 and his average to .321, and there was no longer any doubt that he belonged in the majors.

The Brooklyn Dodgers dominated the National League in the 1950s until they moved to Los Angeles, and Snider played a key role on that team. While most of the major players were right-handed batters, Snider swung from the left side and supplied the power for the Dodgers from that side in grand style. He hit 40 or more home runs from 1953 to 1957 and averaged nearly 120 RBIs for each of those five seasons, while hitting well above .300 for three of those years. Snider was also a smooth and graceful center fielder. Few balls got past the "Duke of Flatbush," and he had a strong and accurate throwing arm that kept many runners from taking an extra base.

Snider was also at his best in the World Series. Even though the Yankees beat the Dodgers in four of their five matchups between 1949–1956, Snider shined in the Fall Classic each year. He hit .300 or better four times and had 11 home runs and 26 RBIs.

When the Dodgers moved to Los Angeles after the 1957 season, Snider lost much of his home run potential because of the Los Angeles Coliseum's deep right field. Even still, he managed to hit over .300 during his first two seasons there. A longtime favorite of Brooklyn fans, Snider returned to New York in 1963 to play for the Mets. He finished up his career the next year with the San Francisco Giants.

He was inducted into the Hall of Fame in 1980.

Durable and dependable, the stylish right-hander **ROBIN ROBERTS** was one of the National League's leading pitchers during the 1950s.

A native of Springfield, Illinois, Roberts was a superb high school basketball player and attended Michigan State University on a basketball scholarship. However, eventually he discovered the college's baseball diamond, and his career as a pitcher began in earnest. After throwing two no-hitters at Michigan State, he was a highly sought-after talent. The Philadelphia Phillies signed him for $25,000 in 1948.

The Phillies were slowly building a good ballclub, and Roberts became a major part of their pennant hopes. In 1949, he won 15 games as the team rose to third place. The following year, he won his twentieth game in the final game of the season as Philadelphia's "Whiz Kids" edged the Brooklyn Dodgers for first place. He was the first Phillies pitcher since 1917 to win 20 games. In the World Series that year, Roberts lost a heartbreaking 2–1 ten-inning decision to the Yankees, who went on to sweep the Series in four games.

Even as the Phillies were regressing in the standings in subsequent years, Roberts became one of the top pitchers in the National League. In 1952, he won 28 games, which was a number no other National League pitcher would reach for the rest of the twentieth century.

For the next three seasons, he led the league each year in wins with 23.

Although he did lead the league in strikeouts twice, Roberts was never a particularly hard thrower. Relying on control and a variety of pitches to record outs, his philosophy was to pitch well enough to win. If he had a big lead in a game, he'd take something off his fastball and let batters try to hit it. But

Roberts's real strength was in his durability and consistency. He led the league five straight seasons in complete games—an average of 28 per year—and innings pitched, surpassing 300 each season.

Roberts then led the league in losses in 1956 and 1957, although this was not entirely his fault. The Phillies were already on their way to becoming the worst team in the league, and in 1961, he fell to a 1–10 record. Philadelphia finished last for the fourth straight year. Roberts then went to the Baltimore Orioles in the American League, where he recovered his winning ways for three fine seasons.

Roberts returned briefly to the National League with the Houston Astros and the Chicago Cubs and then retired after the 1966 season, finishing his career with 286 lifetime wins. Roberts was inducted into the Hall of Fame in 1976.

A crafty left-hander who was at his best in big games, **WHITEY FORD** was the ace of the pitching staff on the great New York Yankees rosters of the 1950s and early 1960s.

Edward Charles Ford was born in New York City in 1926 and was given the nickname "Whitey" because of his light blond hair. A first baseman and pitcher in high school, when his hitting remained weak, he abandoned first base to concentrate on pitching.

New York Yankees scouts spotted him in a sandlot game, and the team outbid the Boston Red Sox and the Brooklyn Dodgers for his services. The Yankees sent him to one of their Pennsylvania farm teams, where he was tutored by their former pitching legend Lefty Gomez (see no. 38).

Under Gomez's guidance, Ford developed into an impressive pitcher after only a few minor league seasons. The Yankees called him up in the middle of the 1950 campaign, and he posted a 9–1 record for the rest of the season. Then, he won the climactic fourth game of the World Series that year as the Yankees completed a sweep over the Philadelphia Phillies.

Ford was called into military service for two years, and when he returned for the 1953 season, he picked up where he left off, posting an 18–6 record and leading the Yankees to their fifth consecutive world championship. He quickly became the top guy on the pitching staff, winning 16, 18, and 19 games over the following three years. Manager Casey Stengel kept Ford fresh by never letting him pitch more than around 250 innings per season. The result was that Ford compiled winning percentages well above .600 in every season up until 1960 except for one.

Always serious when he took the mound, Ford was known to enjoy a good time after hours, and he frequently was out on the town celebrating victories with his Yankees buddies and teammates, Mickey Mantle and Billy Martin. And they had plenty to celebrate: New York won eight pennants and six world championships during the 1950s.

When Ralph Houk became manager for the Yankees in 1961, he abandoned Stengel's 250-inning yardstick for Ford. The increase in innings pitched resulted in Ford's two greatest seasons: 25–4 in 1961, and 24–7 in 1963. The Yankees won five more pennants and two World Series from 1960 to 1964.

In all, Ford appeared in eleven World Series with the Yankees, and he holds the record for the most wins with 10 and strikeouts with 94.

Ford retired after the 1967 season with a lifetime record of 236–106 and a .690 winning percentage, which is, to date, the third best in history. He was inducted into the Hall of Fame in 1974.

When **MICKEY MANTLE** first burst onto the baseball scene in 1951, there were many people who thought he might become the greatest all-around player in history. That never happened, but Mantle remains one of the most talented and popular players ever to put on a major league uniform.

Born in Spavinaw, Oklahoma, Mantle was named after famous catcher Mickey Cochrane by his baseball-loving father. His father started preparing him for a baseball career before he even began school, including teaching him how to switch-hit.

Blessed with great strength and blazing speed, Mantle signed a contract out of high school to play with the New York Yankees. After going up and down between the Yankees and the minors in 1951, Mantle became Joe DiMaggio's replacement in center field beginning with the 1952 season.

His first three years, he put up solid but rather unspectacular numbers: a .300 average, 25–30 home runs, and 80–100 RBIs. He did this all the while playing under the pressure of replacing the legendary DiMaggio as the next "superstar" for the Yankees.

Then, beginning in 1955, Mantle began to live up to his highly regarded potential. That season he hit .306 and led the league with 37 homers. In 1956, he won the first of three Most Valuable Player (MVP) Awards and a Triple Crown, with a .353 average, 52 homers, and 130 RBIs.

In 1958, he slammed 42 homers to lead the league again, and in 1961, in the famed "home run duel" with Roger Maris, he hit 54 homers.

Like Babe Ruth, many of Mantle's homers were "tape measure" blasts that wound up more than 500 feet from the home plate. And, like Ruth, he was eventually idolized in New York and around the country by millions of fans, who admired his ability and determination to play through many frequent and painful injuries.

However, there were also downsides to his career. In addition to his injuries, Mantle lived a hard life off the field. He never took care of his body and was known to drink heavily. Much of this stemmed from the fact that he believed he was fated to die young like his father and grandfather, so he lived every day like it was his last.

During Mantle's career with the Yankees, the team won twelve pennants and seven world championships, and he was a major reason for their success. When he retired, he held the World Series career records for home runs with 18, runs scored with 42, and RBIs with 40.

Mantle's last good year was in 1964, when he hit .303, with 35 homers and 111 RBIs, although he hung on through the 1968 season. He was elected to the Hall of Fame in 1974.

Known for his relentless cheerfulness and sheer love of the game, **ERNIE BANKS** set new standards for hitting and slugging as a National League shortstop during the 1950s.

Born in Dallas, Texas, in 1931, Banks was a high school athletic star. However, it was his slugging in a church softball league that alerted scouts, who signed him to play for the semipro Amarillo Colts in 1948.

Two years later, Banks was playing for the Kansas City Monarchs of the Negro American League. After a two-year army stint, Banks returned to the Monarchs. With the integration of the major leagues, the era of Black baseball was dying out, and several major league clubs wanted to sign Banks. However, the Monarchs' owner would only agree to let him go to a club that put him directly on the major league roster. When the Chicago Cubs agreed, the Monarchs sold Banks's contract to them, and he became their first Black player.

The club did not know it at the time, but

it had signed the one player whose brilliance would outshine all others in a Cubs' uniform. Year after year, as the team had one mediocre season after another, Banks remained the sole bright spot with his hitting and fielding.

In 1955, his second year with the club, Banks blasted 44 home runs—a record for a shortstop. In 1958, he hit .313 and led the league with 47 homers and 129 runs batted in. The next year, he hit .304, with 45 homers and once again led the league in RBIs with 143.

Both times, Banks was voted the league's Most Valuable Player (MVP). In 1958, he became the first man from a team under .500 to win the award, and in 1959, he became the first player in league history to win back-to-back awards.

As shortstop, Banks was a fine fielder. He led the league in fielding percentage three times in eight seasons, and in 1960, he won a Gold Glove Award. In 1961, injuries began to slow him down, and the Cubs asked him to change positions. After a brief try in the outfield, he moved permanently to first base in 1962, and became a fine fielder there as well.

Banks became known as "Mr. Cub" and was always upbeat and smiling, even though he never played in a World Series, and the Cubs were rarely in contention. His well-known saying, "What a great day for baseball. Let's play two," endeared him not only to Cub fans, but to baseball lovers everywhere.

Banks retired following the 1971 season with 512 lifetime home runs. He was inducted into the Hall of Fame in 1977.

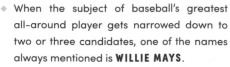

When the subject of baseball's greatest all-around player gets narrowed down to two or three candidates, one of the names always mentioned is **WILLIE MAYS**.

Mays could do everything on the diamond. He could hit for both average and power, steal bases, and field spectacularly—and he had a strong, accurate throwing arm. In his prime, he was simply one of the most complete ballplayers of all time.

Born in Westfield, Alabama, Mays showed his baseball talent early—he was playing with adults on his father's steel mill team when he was just fourteen years old. By 1947, he was starring with the Birmingham Black Barons of the Negro Leagues.

That same year, Jackie Robinson (see no. 48) broke baseball's color line and made it to the major leagues. That opened the door for other Black players, and Mays was prime material for the majors. The New York Giants signed him in 1950 and sent him to the minors.

Mays was hitting an astounding .477 for Minneapolis in 1951 when the Giants called him up. However, he struggled initially, and he tearfully asked Giants manager Leo Durocher to send him back down. Durocher stuck with him, though, and when Mays blasted a home run off Warren Spahn, he was on his way to the top.

Mays finished the season with a .274 average and 20 homers while winning Rookie of the Year honors. He helped spark the Giants' amazing comeback from 13 1/2 games back to overtake the Brooklyn Dodgers for the National League pennant.

Mays missed the next two seasons while serving in the military, and when he returned in 1954, he was outstanding. He hit .345 with 41 homers and 110 RBIs, won the Most Valuable Player (MVP) Award, and led the Giants to another pennant and a four-game sweep over the Cleveland Indians in the World Series.

For the next twelve years, Mays was the most dominant player in the game. He led the league in homers four times, twice hitting over 50. He consistently hit over .300, had more than 100 RBIs nine times, and led the league in stolen bases four years in a row.

The "Say Hey Kid" was also a peerless fielder. With his hat flying off, he thrilled fans with his famous basket catch to corral fly balls. His unbelievable back-to-home plate catch of a Vic Wertz deep drive in the 1954 World Series is considered the greatest catch in baseball history. He won twelve Gold Glove Awards during his career.

Elected to the Hall of Fame in 1979, Mays retired after twenty-two seasons with a .302 lifetime batting average, 660 home runs, 1,903 RBIs, and 338 stolen bases.

Although **MAURY WILLS** never slugged 450-foot homers or threw blazing fastballs, he nevertheless revolutionized baseball by reintroducing the stolen base as a devastating offensive weapon in the 1960s.

Maurice Morning Wills was born in Washington, DC, in 1932. Signed by the Brooklyn Dodgers at seventeen years old in 1950, Wills languished in the minors for nearly ten years because he was a weak hitter. In the spring of 1959, the Dodgers thought so little of Wills that they traded him conditionally to the Detroit Tigers, who did not see much in him either and promptly returned him.

Later that year, the Dodgers' starting shortstop, Don Zimmer, broke his toe, and the desperate team finally gave Wills a shot. Much to their surprise, he did a good job, batting .260 and stealing 7 bases in 83 games. In their World Series victory against the Chicago White Sox, Wills hit .250 and stole as many bases—one—as the reigning king of stolen bases, Chicago's Luis Aparicio.

The following year, Wills became the Dodgers' starting shortstop, hitting .295 and setting a team record with 50 steals. In 1961, he hit .282 and again led the league in steals with 35. However, Wills was only getting started. In 1962, he really hit his stride, hitting .299 and stealing 104 bases—breaking Ty Cobb's record of 96 steals that had lasted nearly fifty years. Wills was voted the National League's Most Valuable Player (MVP) that year as the Dodgers tied for first place but lost the three-game playoff to the San Francisco Giants.

Wills led the National League in steals for the next three seasons as well. He was a major weapon in the Dodgers' offense, an attack that featured almost no power and relied heavily on Wills's ability to get on, steal a base or two, and score on a single or sacrifice fly. Combined with the great pitching of Sandy Koufax and Don Drysdale, this formula enabled them to win the pennant and the World Series in both 1963 and 1965.

By 1966, the years of sliding and constant jarring contact with the ground had taken its toll on Wills, turning the lower half of his body into a mass of bruises. In 1967, he was traded to the Pittsburgh Pirates, where he continued to steal bases but with significantly dropped numbers from what they had been earlier in the decade.

Wills retired following the 1972 season with 586 lifetime steals. He had an unsuccessful stint as manager of the Seattle Mariners in 1980 and 1981. However, the skinny young man from Washington with the flying feet would always be remembered for bringing the excitement of the stolen base back to baseball in the 1960s.

With a cannon for an arm and a sweet swing that made him one of baseball's best hitters, **ROBERTO CLEMENTE** was one of the greatest outfielders ever to play the game. Roberto Walker Clemente was born in Carolina, Puerto Rico. When he was barely nineteen years old, he was already starring for the Santurce Crabbers, a professional team in Puerto Rico's Winter League.

The Brooklyn Dodgers signed him to a contract with a fat $10,000 bonus in 1954. At the time, baseball rules required that any player receiving a bonus had to play in the majors or else they could be drafted by another team at the end of the year. The Dodgers placed him with their Montreal farm team, hoping that no other team would discover him there. However, a scout for the Pittsburgh Pirates noticed his talent, and the team signed him at the end of the season.

Clemente's first five years were solid, if unspectacular. Then, in 1960, he hit .314, and that began a streak of eight straight seasons where he hit over .300. That year he helped the Pirates win the pennant and then upset the favored Yankees in the World Series. Clemente had nine hits and batted .310 in the Series.

Throughout the 1960s, Clemente continued his brilliant play. He won four batting titles during the decade, and in 1966, he won the league's Most Valuable Player (MVP) Award. Despite this success, he still played in the shadow of more publicized stars, such as Hank Aaron and Willie Mays.

Clemente led the Pirates to another pennant in 1971, and then, in the World Series that year, he cemented his reputation as a great clutch player. The Pirates were underdogs to the powerful Baltimore Orioles, and Clemente led the team back from a two-game deficit to win the Series in seven games. He hit .414 and fielded magnificently, winning the Series MVP Award.

In his final game of the 1972 season, Clemente notched his 3,000th hit, becoming only the eleventh player in baseball history to attain that mark. That year, he also won his twelfth straight Gold Glove Award.

Clemente was a great humanitarian, proud of his Spanish heritage, and determined to help those in need. When Nicaragua was hit by a devastating earthquake in December 1972, Clemente organized a relief effort that sent supplies to disaster victims. When he heard that the corrupt government was stealing the supplies, he traveled with the next planeload to deliver the supplies himself. Tragically, on December 31, 1972, the plane crashed into the ocean, killing everyone on board.

To honor Clemente, baseball suspended the normal five-year waiting period and inducted him into the Hall of Fame in 1973.

ROGER MARIS broke baseball's most hallowed record in 1961, but despite the accomplishment, he had a miserable time doing it.

Roger Eugene Maris was born in Hibbing, Minnesota. An outstanding high school athlete, he spent time with both the Cleveland Indians and the Kansas City A's before going to the Yankees in 1960. That year, he hit .283 with 39 home runs and 112 RBIs, and he also won the American League's Most Valuable Player (MVP) Award.

The following year, Maris got off to a slow start. But he soon got hot, and by midsummer, both he and teammate Mickey Mantle were hitting home runs at a startling pace.

Soon it became apparent that both Maris and Mantle had a chance to shatter Babe Ruth's record of 60 homers in one season. Sportswriters began peppering them with questions about whether they thought they could do it. Mantle, much more accustomed to New York publicity, was able

to shrug it off. The reserved and shy Maris began wilting under the relentless pressure.

All through the summer, Mantle and Maris dueled for the home run lead. Mantle, by now the acknowledged leader of the Yankees for many seasons, was the popular choice to break the mark. When he went down with an injury in September with 54 homers, the glare of the spotlight shifted firmly to Maris. He responded by withdrawing even further, being abrupt with reporters and looking so nerve-wracked that his hair began to fall out.

To add to the pressure, Maris had to chase the record under an artificial deadline imposed by Commissioner Ford Frick, once a close friend of Babe Ruth. Frick ruled that to legitimately break the record, Maris had to do it in 154 games—the number Ruth had played in—not 162, which was the number of games Maris would play in the new schedule for 1961.

While Maris failed to break the record within Frick's deadline, he did finally catch Ruth and pass him—hitting his sixty-first homer in the final game of the season.

Throughout his career, Maris was a solid hitter and a superb outfielder, arguably one of the best right fielders in Yankee history. However, after his performance in 1961, expectations ran so high that anything Maris accomplished later never seemed good enough.

Maris spent several more unhappy seasons in New York, putting up decent numbers but also fighting injuries and suffering boos from fans who expected much more from him. He was traded to the St. Louis Cardinals in 1967. He led them to two straight National League pennants before retiring. His record lasted thirty-seven years—longer than Ruth's—until Mark McGwire broke it in 1998.

HANK AARON will forever be known as the man who broke Babe Ruth's career home run record. However, he should also be remembered as the steadiest and most consistent hitter of his era, and one of the greatest all-around players the game has ever seen.

Aaron was born in Mobile, Alabama, and began his pro career as an eighteen-year-old shortstop with the Indianapolis Clowns of the Negro Leagues. However, Black baseball was virtually finished, and the Boston Braves of the National League signed him the following year. He spent two years in the minors and learned to play the outfield. In 1954, with the Braves beginning their second season in Milwaukee, he became the team's left fielder.

Aaron hit .280 that year with 13 home runs. The following year, Aaron switched to right field, where he became a fixture for the next sixteen seasons. Although never a spectacular outfielder, he was sure-handed and reliable and had an accurate arm.

With Aaron in right field, and such players as Eddie Mathews, Warren Spahn, and Lew Burdette, the Braves produced a powerhouse team in the late 1950s. They won the pennant in 1957 and 1958 and won the world championship in 1957.

Although not a particularly big man for a power hitter, Aaron's quick wrists were legendary. He often swung at the ball so late that he appeared to be hitting it right out of the catcher's glove. His ability to wait on pitches until the last moment produced a remarkably consistent career. He hit .300 or better fourteen times, slugged 40 or more homers eight times, and drove in more than 100 runs eleven times. His 2,297 lifetime RBI mark also broke Babe Ruth's career record. Aaron led the league in home runs and RBIs four times, won the batting title twice, and was the league's Most Valuable Player (MVP) in 1957.

By 1973, it became clear that if Aaron remained healthy, he would surpass Babe Ruth in career home runs. As he got closer to the record, Aaron stoically endured a great deal of racial abuse that included death threats, although the public was not made aware of it. His dignified demeanor amid the media frenzy leading up to the record homer typified Aaron's career. He finally out-performed Ruth on April 8, 1974, with his 715th lifetime homer, and all of baseball celebrated his tremendous feat.

Aaron retired after the 1976 season with a .305 batting average, a record 6,856 total bases, and 755 lifetime home runs. Some people consider "Hammerin' Hank" to be the greatest right-handed hitter in the history of the game. He was inducted into the Hall of Fame in 1982.

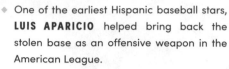

One of the earliest Hispanic baseball stars, **LUIS APARICIO** helped bring back the stolen base as an offensive weapon in the American League.

A native of Maracaibo, Venezuela, Aparicio had baseball talent in his veins. His father was considered Venezuela's greatest shortstop, although he never got the chance to play in the majors. Aparicio gained recognition as a top-flight prospect in his native country as a youngster, and the Cleveland Indians were very interested in signing him. However, when they dawdled, the Chicago White Sox swooped in and scooped him up for themselves.

In spring training of 1956, the White Sox thought so highly of Aparicio's talent that they handed him the shortstop job which a trade had left open. Aparicio rewarded the White Sox's faith in him by hitting .266 with a league-leading 21 stolen bases and winning the Rookie of the Year Award.

That began a nine-year streak in which

he led the league in steals—a record that still has not been broken. His personal best was 57 steals in 1964.

Even more importantly, Aparicio made the stolen base popular again as a part of baseball strategy after it had been dormant for many years. The 1950s were a time of stagnation in baseball offensive strategy, as teams tended to wait for a home run rather than use speed and try to manufacture a run. In 1954, for example, Jackie Jensen led the American League in stolen bases with 22—a good month's total for Ty Cobb or other base stealers of the past.

Aparicio changed all that. Like Maury Wills in the National League in the 1960s, Aparicio proved that you didn't need a big hit to get a man into scoring position on second base. He would get a single or walk, followed by a steal. Both men helped pave the wave for future base bandits such as Lou Brock and Rickey Henderson.

Aparicio teamed with second baseman Nellie Fox to give the "Go-Go" White Sox a winning keystone combination. In 1959, the two led Chicago to the pennant, running the rest of the league dizzy. The Sox were last in the league in homers, but first in stolen bases.

Later Aparicio played with the Baltimore Orioles and the Boston Red Sox before retiring in 1974 with 506 lifetime stolen bases. He played in more games, threw out more batters, and was involved in more double plays than any shortstop in baseball history. A slick fielder, he also won nine Gold Glove Awards. In 1984, he was elected to the Hall of Fame.

67 AL KALINE

1934–2020

◆ The youngest player ever to win a batting title, **AL KALINE** was a model of consistency both at the plate and in the field throughout his entire twenty-two-year career with the Detroit Tigers.

Kaline was born in Baltimore, Maryland, to a baseball happy family. His father, grandfather, and uncles all played semipro ball. A star in high school, Kaline batted .488 as a senior and had scouts flocking to his door. Eventually, he signed a bonus contract with the Detroit Tigers. Under the baseball rules at the time, that contract meant that Kaline had to stay on the big league roster for two years, or Detroit could lose him. Consequently, Kaline never played a day in the minor leagues.

Kaline played in only 30 games as a rookie in 1953, but the Tigers were impressed enough that, the next season, they made him their starting right fielder. Kaline hit .276 that season and really blossomed in 1955. He had 200 hits to lead the league and batted .340 to win the batting title. He also had 27 home runs and 102 RBIs—all before twenty-one years old.

Though he never matched the brilliance of that first year, Kaline did develop into a superb player both offensively and defensively. He hit over .300 eight more times and reached the magic plateau of 3,000 hits with 3,007. He also hit 399 career home runs and had 1,583 RBIs.

Kaline was also a sensational outfielder. He had excellent reflexes, was smooth and quick, and possessed a cannon arm. Few runners dared to try and take an extra base on any ball hit his way.

Unfortunately, throughout most of Kaline's career, the Tigers were an also-ran team. However, Detroit finally won the American League pennant in 1968 and faced the St. Louis Cardinals in the World Series. Kaline had broken his leg during the season and was just rounding into shape for the Series. Desperate to get him into the lineup, Tiger manager Mayo Smith gambled that Kaline's replacement during the season, outfielder Mickey Stanley, would be able to play shortstop so that Kaline could play the outfield. The ploy worked like a charm for Detroit. Stanley played well at short, and Kaline hit .379 and drove in eight runs as the Tigers beat St. Louis.

As he slowed down in his last few years, Kaline switched to first base so his bat could stay in the lineup. A soft-spoken and modest man, Kaline was always one of Detroit's most popular players. After he retired in 1974, he became one of the team's broadcasters. He was inducted into the Hall of Fame in 1980.

One thing can certainly be said for **FRANK ROBINSON**, and that is that he never played favorites. After making life miserable for National League pitchers for ten years, he went over to the American League and did the same there for several more seasons.

Born in Beaumont, Texas, Robinson was a three-sport star in high school. One of his baseball teammates was Vada Pinson, who would later play alongside him in the major leagues. In 1953, Robinson signed a contract with the Cincinnati Reds of the National League.

After tearing up the minor leagues, Robinson joined the Reds in 1956 and immediately made an impact. He won Rookie of the Year honors, hitting .290, leading the league with 122 runs scored, and smashing 38 home runs, which tied a league record for rookie homers. Over the next four seasons, Robinson averaged more than 30 homers and 90 RBIs each year.

Then in 1961, he hit .324, with 37 homers

and 124 RBIs, as he helped lead Cincinnati to the pennant, and won the National League's Most Valuable Player (MVP) Award. Robinson continued to play great ball for the Reds up through the mid-1960s, but at the end of the 1965 season, the Reds traded him to the Baltimore Orioles in the American League. Cincinnati's general manager, while acknowledging that Robinson was only thirty, claimed that he was an "old thirty."

It was one of the worst trades in baseball history. In 1966, Robinson proceeded to win the American League's Triple Crown by hitting .316, with 49 homers and 122 RBIs. He was named the league's MVP, becoming the first person to win the award in both leagues. Robinson's offensive heroics helped power the Orioles to the pennant and a four-game sweep over the Los Angeles Dodgers in the World Series.

With Robinson's leadership, the Orioles were perennial contenders. They won three straight pennants, from 1969 to 1971, and another world championship in 1970. In addition to his great ability, Robinson had a combative, aggressive personality that frequently infused his teammates with a never-say-die attitude. In 1975, Robinson made baseball history again when he became player-manager of the Cleveland Indians as the first Black manager in the game. However, he couldn't infuse the lackluster Indians with any of his trademark fire and was let go in 1977.

Robinson retired as a player in 1976. A lifetime .294 hitter, he had 2,943 hits, 586 homers, and 1,812 RBIs. He later managed the San Francisco Giants and the Orioles in the 1980s. After more than ten years away from being in the dugout, he went back in to manage the Montreal Expos from 2002 to 2006.

Robinson was inducted into the Hall of Fame in 1982.

During the 1960s and early 1970s, when great pitching seemed to be everywhere, **BOB GIBSON** was probably the most dominating right-handed hurler on the field.

Ironically, as a youth in Omaha, Nebraska, a heart murmur and asthma made it seem as if an athletic career was an impossible dream for Gibson. However, showing his hallmark competitive nature, he overcame both health problems to become a four-sport star in high school.

Baseball was his first love, and in 1957, Gibson signed with the St. Louis Cardinals. He joined St. Louis in 1959 and spent two seasons as a reliever and part-time starter without really distinguishing himself. Then, in 1961, he became a member of the Cardinals' starting rotation.

Gibson won 13 games that year—the second most on the staff. The following season, he won 15, had an excellent earned run average (ERA) of 2.85, and struck out 208 batters. It was the first of nine seasons he would compile more than 200 strikeouts.

In 1964, Gibson won 19 games and led the Cardinals to the World Series, where he won two more in the team's seven-game victory over the Yankees. He won 20 games in each of the next two seasons and was on his way to another great year in 1967, when a line drive broke his right leg and he missed 56 games. However, he recovered in time for the World Series against the Boston Red Sox, and he was outstanding. He pitched three complete game victories, including the decisive seventh game, giving up only 14 hits and 3 earned runs.

The following year, Gibson had one of the most dominating years any pitcher ever had, winning 22 games, striking out 268 batters, throwing 13 shutouts, and posting an unheard of 1.12 ERA. He won both the Cy Young Award and Most Valuable Player

(MVP) Award that year. The Cardinals made it to the World Series again, and Gibson won two more games, including Game 1, where he struck out a record 17 Detroit Tiger batters. Unfortunately, he lost a close decision in Game 7. Overall, during his career, Gibson won seven World Series games.

Gibson won 20 games again in 1969. In 1970, he had a record of 23–7 with 274 strikeouts, and he won another Cy Young Award.

A ferocious competitor, Gibson was an intimidating presence on the mound as a tall, lanky, and scowling figure with a blazing fastball. And he was not averse to knocking a batter down if he crowded too close to the plate.

Gibson retired after the 1975 season with 251 lifetime victories. He was inducted into the Hall of Fame in 1981.

It took **SANDY KOUFAX** years to perfect his craft, and his career was prematurely shortened due to an injury. Still, while he took the mound during the 1960s, Koufax reigned as baseball's best pitcher.

Born in Brooklyn, New York, Koufax excelled as a youngster in basketball rather than in baseball. He attended the University of Cincinnati on a basketball scholarship in 1953. He also joined the baseball team, where he played both first base and pitched. Koufax was a poor hitter, but he showed such promise as a pitcher that several teams expressed interest in him. His hometown Brooklyn Dodgers team signed him for $20,000, and he left school to join them.

At that time, Koufax was considered a "bonus baby," and the rules stipulated that he had to stay on the major league roster in order to stay on the team that recruited him. Thus, while he showed occasional flashes of brilliance, he developed very slowly. For the first six years, he struggled with wildness, and his record only amounted to 36–40.

Then, in spring training in 1961, Dodger

catcher Norm Sherry suggested that Koufax slow his delivery, ease up on his fastballs, and mix in more curves. That simple advice transformed an average pitcher into a great one.

Koufax went 18–13 that year and led the league with 269 strikeouts. In 1962, he racked up a 14–7 record before an injury shortened his season. Then he began a four-year stretch when he simply overwhelmed National League teams.

From 1963 to 1966, Koufax's won-lost record was 97–27, a .782 percentage. His yearly marks were 25–5, 19–5, 26–8, and 27–9. He pitched 1,192 innings, struck out 1,228 batters, threw 31 shutouts, and had an earned run average (ERA) under 2.00 in three of those years. A stylish southpaw with a blazing fastball and a wicked curve, Koufax pitched four no-hitters and one perfect game. In 1963, he won both the National League's Cy Young Award and Most Valuable Player (MVP) Award.

Koufax and Don Drysdale provided an unbeatable one-two pitching tandem that led the Los Angeles Dodgers to three pennants and two world championships in the mid-1960s. Koufax was at his best in big games. He won four Word Series contests, including the championship-clinching games twice. In the 1965 Series, he pitched the seventh game on only two days of rest and shut out the Minnesota Twins on three hits while striking out ten. His career World Series ERA was an astounding 0.95.

After the 1966 season, and still at the peak of his career, Koufax stunned baseball by announcing his retirement at the age of thirty. Suffering from an arthritic elbow, he was told that further pitching could cause permanent injury to his arm.

Koufax was inducted into the Hall of Fame in 1972.

Combining a fierce demeanor with an overpowering fastball, **DON DRYSDALE** was one of the top pitchers of his generation.

Born in Van Nuys, California, Drysdale didn't become a pitcher until his senior year in high school. However, once the young Drysdale did start pitching, he quickly became a star. The Brooklyn Dodgers scouted and signed him in 1954.

Drysdale pitched two years in the minors, racking up modest won-lost marks of 8–5 and 11–11. Despite his so-so record, he was promoted to the parent club in 1956. Once on the major league roster, he fell under the influence of veteran hurler Sal Maglie, who was finishing up a solid career at that time with the Dodgers.

Maglie was nicknamed "The Barber" because of his tendency to pitch inside and give batters "a close shave." He imparted this strategy about moving batters away from the plate to Drysdale. Apparently, the young pitcher paid very close attention. After posting only a 5–5 record his first year in 1957, Drysdale improved dramatically to a 17–9 mark the next season. He also began to develop a reputation as someone willing to pitch inside, even to the point of hitting batters.

It was in 1959 and 1960 that Drysdale emerged as a dominant pitcher. The Dodgers had moved to Los Angeles in 1958, and Drysdale was now pitching just a few miles from where he had grown up. Obviously, being close to home agreed with him. He led the league in strikeouts both years with 242 and 246, respectively, and compiled won-lost records of 17–13 and 15–14.

In 1962, Drysdale had his greatest season; he was 25–9, with 314 innings pitched and 232 strikeouts—all league-leading marks. Those totals earned him the Cy Young Award. The following year he was 19–17 and

hurled a shutout in the Dodgers' four-game sweep over the Yankees in the World Series.

Big and strong, Drysdale was an intimidating presence on the mound. He had a sweeping sidearm motion that, combined with his reputation for wildness, prevented batters from digging in at the plate against him. By the midsixties, he and left-handed Dodger ace Sandy Koufax provided the most potent one-two pitching duo in the league. Together, they led the team to three pennants and two world championships during that decade.

In 1968, Drysdale threw a string of 58 2/3 consecutive scoreless innings, breaking the previous record of 56 held by Walter Johnson. In 1988, the record was broken by another Dodger, Orel Hershiser.

Drysdale retired after the 1969 season with 209 lifetime victories. He was elected to the Hall of Fame in 1984.

With his huge lumberjack arms and bulging muscles, **HARMON KILLEBREW** was a fearsome sight to behold standing at the plate.

The strong Idahoan man, nicknamed "Killer," became the leading right-handed home run hitter in American League history by the time he retired, having belted 573 career round-trippers. Yet his nickname belied his soft-spoken, almost shy demeanor, and he was frequently overlooked in the media for flashier players even as he was consistently launching home runs out of ballparks.

Harmon Clayton Killebrew was born in Payette, Idaho. Although he didn't begin playing baseball until his late teens, he quickly made up for lost time and was soon being hailed as the strongest player in the West. Idaho Senator Herman Walker wrote a note about Killebrew's talents to the Washington Senators' owner Clark Griffith. When Griffith dispatched a scout to see Killebrew play with his high school team, he

hit a 485-foot home run. The scout subsequently found out that Killebrew was hitting a "mere" .847. Needless to say, the Senators immediately signed Killebrew.

Killebrew then spent the next several seasons moving back and forth from the Senators to the minors before finally getting the chance to play regularly in 1959. All he did in his first full season was hit 42 homers to lead the American League.

Harmon Killebrew was more than ready to play in the major leagues. Over the next twelve years, he produced 40-home-run seasons with startling ease and consistency, only to break that number seven more times. He peaked at 49 in both 1964 and 1969. In 1969, he also drove in 140 RBIs and had a .276 batting average that won him the league's Most Valuable Player (MVP) Award.

In 1965, when the Senators, now playing as the transplanted Minnesota Twins, won the pennant, Killebrew hit 25 homers and drove in 75 runs despite being plagued by injuries.

Although he was a second baseman when he first went up to the big leagues, Killebrew primarily played first and third base during his career. A quiet man who preferred returning to his native Idaho for off-season hunting and fishing, Killebrew was beloved by fans in both Washington and Minnesota for his demeanor and solid professionalism.

After a knee injury slowed him down and the Twins released him, he played one final season for the Kansas City Royals in 1975 before retiring. Killebrew played in more than 2,400 games over his career. Along with his 573 home runs, he had 2,086 hits and 1,584 RBIs. He was inducted into the Hall of Fame in 1984.

It was the 1970 World Series, and the Baltimore Orioles' third baseman, **BROOKS ROBINSON**, had just made another in a series of spectacular fielding displays against the Cincinnati Reds.

Reds' catcher Johnny Bench, who as a right-handed hitter, had already been victimized several times by Robinson. This time, he watched the third baseman's latest incredible play and just shook his head.

"I will become a left-handed hitter to keep the ball away from that guy," he vowed.

Bench was only learning what hitters in the American League had known for years. And after the Orioles had beaten them in five games, thanks in no small part to Robinson's brilliant defensive play, Cincinnati understood why Robinson was nicknamed "Hoover"—as in the vacuum cleaner that sucks up everything.

That was Brooks Calbert Robinson—possibly the greatest defensive third baseman baseball has ever seen. Born in Little Rock, Arkansas, Robinson was discovered while playing second base in a church league. He was an extremely slow runner, and when the Orioles took one look at his lack of speed, they told him to forget second base and play third.

Robinson became the Orioles' regular third baseman in 1960. That year, he hit .294 with 88 runs batted in. In 1964, he had perhaps his finest offensive season. He batted .317 with a career-high 28 homers and a league leading 118 RBIs. He was also named the American League's Most Valuable Player (MVP) that year.

In 1966, the Orioles won their first pennant and World Series. Robinson hit 23 homers and drove in 100 runs that season. Altogether, he played on four pennant-winning and two world championship-earning teams. He was donned MVP of the 1970 World Series, in which he hit .429. Along with Frank Robinson and a solid pitching staff, Brooks Robinson was one of the main cogs of the great Oriole teams of the late 1960s and early 1970s.

However, while Robinson always put up respectable offensive numbers, it was his defense that brought amazement from both players and fans alike. Balls seemed to magically find their way into his glove, and he had a habit of making spectacular plays look routine. It became a common sight to see Robinson on his knees, firing the ball across the diamond to first base to beat a runner. To compensate for his lack of speed, Robinson used his wit and reflexes to dive to his right across the foul line or to his left into the hole, once again robbing hitters of potential singles and doubles.

Robinson won the Gold Glove Award fifteen times. He retired in 1977, after a twenty-three-year career, all with the Orioles. He was inducted into the Hall of Fame in 1983.

◆ With an assortment of five pitches and an impossibly high leg kick that reportedly stretched up to the sky, **JUAN MARICHAL**, with a total of 191 games won, outperformed any other pitcher in baseball in the 1960s.

Juan Antonio Marichal Sanchez was born in Laguna Verde in the Dominican Republic in 1937. He played baseball as a youth and was scouted by the San Francisco Giants, who signed him to a contract in 1958.

The Giants sent Marichal to their Midwest League farm team at Michigan City, Indiana, where he immediately thrived. He led the league with 21 wins and a 1.87 earned run average (ERA). Brought up to the Giants in 1960, Marichal posted a 6–2 record with a 2.66 ERA.

In 1962, Marichal went 18–11 with a 3.36 ERA as he helped pitch the Giants into the World Series against the New York Yankees. He followed that up in 1963 with one of his finest seasons—a record of 25–8, a 2.41 ERA, and a no-hitter against the Houston Colt .45s.

Nicknamed "The Dominican Dandy," Marichal developed into one of the best pitchers in history. Over the next six years, he won more than 20 games five times, recording 25–6 in 1966 and 26–9 in 1968. In those six seasons, his ERA was never higher than 2.76, but he pitched around 300 innings a year and struck out 200 or more hitters each year.

Despite his great success, Marichal's career was somewhat overshadowed during the sixties by two other dominant pitchers: Sandy Koufax and Bob Gibson. It seemed that whenever Marichal had his greatest years, either Koufax or Gibson would have even better seasons. Those two pitchers also benefited from their great successes in the postseason, as the Los Angeles Dodgers and St. Louis Cardinals each went to the World Series three times during the decade. In contrast, Marichal's only Series appearance was in 1962, very early in his career.

The pitcher was also involved in one of baseball's most infamous incidents of the 1960s. In 1965, during another heated Dodger-Giant game, while standing at the plate, Marichal was convinced that Dodger catcher Johnny Roseboro had tried to hit him in the ear when returning the ball to the Dodger pitcher. Marichal attacked Roseboro with his bat, hitting him in the head. Marichal was heavily fined and suspended for the action, and it tainted his reputation for a time. Years later, he made amends with Roseboro, and the two became friends.

Marichal retired in 1975, with a record of 243–142, a lifetime ERA of 2.89, a total of 52 shutouts, and 2,303 cumulative strikeouts. He was elected to the Hall of Fame in 1983.

◆ "The ultimate insult to me was saying that I had to start stealing bases," the St. Louis Cardinals speedster **LOU BROCK** once said. Brock thought of himself as a classic number five or six batter—a long ball hitter with power to find the gaps. How ironic that what Brock considered the ultimate insult would make him famous.

A native of El Dorado, Arkansas, Brock was considered a "can't miss" outfield prospect with the Chicago Cubs. However, when the Cubs wanted a veteran pitcher for their staff, they traded Brock in June 1964 to the Cardinals for former twenty-game winner Ernie Broglio.

The trade ranks as one of the worst in baseball history. Plagued by arm miseries, Broglio won just seven games for the Cubs over the next three years before retiring. Brock, meanwhile, blossomed into a superstar.

When he went over in the trade, Brock hit .348 for St. Louis throughout 103 games and sparked the Cardinals to the pennant and a World Series triumph over the New York Yankees. With Brock providing speed for the offense, the Cardinals would go on to win two more pennants and another world championship in the 1960s. In those three Series appearances, Brock was outstanding—he hit .391 and stole 14 bases, making him first in career World Series thefts.

In 1966, Brock ended Maury Wills's six-year reign as National League stolen base leader when he swiped 74 bases, beginning a four-year streak in which Brock led the league in steals. After having his streak interrupted in 1970, Brock reeled off another four years as league leader, reaching an incredible 118 steals in 1974.

Brock's 118 mark in 1974 broke Wills's twelve-year-old record for stolen bases in a season, which he had set by shattering Ty Cobb's forty-seven-year-old mark. However, Brock wasn't through setting records just yet. In 1977, he broke Cobb's record for lifetime steals, too, swiping the 893rd base of his career during that year.

On the base path, Brock was the ultimate student. With his arms hanging down between his legs and his knees slightly bent, he would study the pitcher intently until he knew his every move. Then, with lightning quickness, he would take off. It was what Brock called "base running arrogance."

During his career, Brock was also a fine hitter, with a lifetime .293 batting average. When he retired in 1979, he had 3,023 hits along with 938 total stolen bases. Lou Brock had "stolen" his way right into the Hall of Fame, into which he was inducted in 1985.

CARL YASTRZEMSKI was asked to perform an impossible task for the Boston Red Sox: replace Ted Williams. And although he didn't quite fulfill those expectations—a player like Williams comes along once every century—Yaz was a great player in his own right.

The son of a Long Island potato farmer and amateur baseball player, Yastrzemski was a good enough player to be pursued by several teams when he was eighteen. He refused them, however, and fulfilled his promise to his father that he would go to college. However, after one year of attending Notre Dame, he decided to become a professional ballplayer. He went to a New York Yankee tryout camp but left when he felt slighted. He ultimately signed with the Red Sox for $100,000.

When Ted Williams retired after the 1960 season, Yastrzemski was moved into his left field spot the next season. He hit .266 and .296 in his first two years and played the difficult left-field position flawlessly. Fenway Park's "Green Monster" wall in left field is infamous for its tricky bounces and caroms, but Yaz played it as if he had been born there.

In 1963, Yastrzemski won the first of his three batting titles with a .321 mark. However, that was just a warm-up for 1967, when Yastrzemski had one of the greatest seasons any ballplayer had ever had.

The Red Sox finished ninth the year before, but in 1967, they won the American League pennant in a wild scramble with three other teams. Yaz won the Triple Crown that year—the last player in the twentieth century to do so—when he batted .326 with 44 homers and 121 RBIs. In the seven-game World Series loss to the St. Louis Cardinals, Yaz hit .400 with three homers.

"For that one season, there could not have been a better baseball player," said Boston manager Dick Williams.

The Red Sox played in one more World Series during Yastrzemski's career in 1975, but they lost that one as well.

Winning a world championship is one of the few goals to elude Yastrzemski.

As he moved effortlessly from the outfield to first base for the Red Sox late in his career, Yaz became recognized as one of the best players of his era. With his bat held in a distinct manner, high over his head but perfectly perpendicular to the ground, he continued to pound the ball. In 1979, he became the first American League player to collect 3,000 hits and 400 homers.

Yastrzemski retired after the 1983 season and was inducted into the Hall of Fame in 1989.

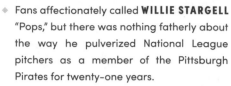

Fans affectionately called **WILLIE STARGELL** "Pops," but there was nothing fatherly about the way he pulverized National League pitchers as a member of the Pittsburgh Pirates for twenty-one years.

Wilver Dornel Stargell was born in Earlsboro, Oklahoma, and grew up in Alameda, California. As a youth, Stargell was a three-sport star in baseball, football, and basketball, and was seriously considering a career on the hardwood. However, as good at basketball as Stargell was, he was that much better at baseball. So when the Pirates came calling in 1959, Stargell was ready to sign.

After a few years in the minors, Stargell went up to the Pirates for good in 1963. He had 11 homers that season, and played in 108 games, alternating between left field and first base. For the rest of his career, Stargell would play both positions. He became the team's established left fielder for years until he finished up his career on first.

Throughout the 1960s, Stargell put up solid though not spectacular numbers. He averaged 25 homers and 86 RBIs during the decade. Stargell's power numbers would no doubt have been even better had he not played half his games in the cavernous Forbes Field, where many of his powerful drives were just long outs. In addition, few people noticed him because he played in the shadow of the Pirates' great right fielder, Roberto Clemente (see no. 63).

Things changed for Stargell when the Pirates moved into the Three Rivers Stadium in 1970. The following year, he blasted 48 homers, with 125 RBIs and a .295 batting average, as he helped drive the Pirates to a pennant and a world championship. After Clemente's tragic death in December 1972, Stargell took over the leadership role on the team.

In 1979, Stargell really captured the attention and affection of baseball fans. The Pirates team, united behind the theme song "We Are Family," swept both a pennant and a World Series triumph. The inspirational leader of the team, Stargell handed out "Stargell Stars" to his teammates when they contributed to a victory. On the field, Stargell's 32 homers and 82 RBIs helped him to become a cowinner of the league's Most Valuable Player (MVP) Award. He was also voted the MVP of both the League Championship Series and the World Series, in which he hit .400.

Stargell retired after the 1982 season and continued to be active in the Pittsburgh community as one of the most beloved sports figures in the city's history. He was inducted into the Hall of Fame in 1988.

A popular and exceptional player during his career, **PETE ROSE** became surrounded in controversy after his playing days concluded. As a result, although he put up Hall of Fame–worthy numbers in his twenty-four years in the majors, he was banned from baseball and Hall of Fame consideration in 1989.

Rose was born in Cincinnati, Ohio, in 1941. He had an uncle who was a scout for the Cincinnati Reds, and he convinced the team to take a chance on his nephew. After a couple of minor league seasons, Rose came to spring training with the Reds in 1963. He pestered the manager Fred Hutchinson to play him, and Hutchinson finally relented. During one game against the Yankees, Rose drew a walk and sprinted down to first base.

"Hey, Charlie Hustle," yelled pitcher Whitey Ford, "Take it easy."

However, Rose didn't take it easy until he had hustled himself into winning the Rookie of the Year Award in 1963. He batted .273 with 170 hits. After declining to .269 in 1964, Rose reeled off nine straight years during which he hit .300 or better. Included in that streak were three National League batting titles. After dropping down to .284 in 1974, Rose then hit more than .300 for five more years in a row. In 1973, he won the league's Most Valuable Player (MVP) Award.

Up until 1979, Rose accomplished these hitting feats with Cincinnati. Along with players such as Joe Morgan and Johnny Bench, he was a vital part of the awesome "Big Red Machine" that won five division championships, three pennants, and back-to-back world championships in 1975 and 1976.

In 1979, Rose joined the Philadelphia Phillies as a free agent, and in 1980, he helped lead them to their only world championship. In addition to being a great leadoff hitter, Rose was a versatile athlete as well, playing various positions in both the infield and outfield throughout his career.

When Rose retired, he left behind a host of records, the most notable being the most career hits—amounting to 4,256—a record he achieved by breaking Ty Cobb's mark of 4,191.

In 1984, Rose returned to the Reds and became a player-manager. He retired as a player in 1986, and in the late 1980s, rumors surfaced that he had bet on baseball games while managing. After an investigation, baseball Commissioner A. Bartlett Giamatti found the rumors to be substantive, and in 1989, he banned Rose from baseball for life, which also precluded him from Hall of Fame consideration. Maintaining his innocence, Rose applied for reinstatement numerous times over the next several years but was continually denied.

♦ With his elbow madly flapping at his side, **JOE MORGAN** looked more like he was trying to fly than hit a baseball. Yet his relatively small size and "chicken-flapping" elbow masked the fact that he was one of the most dangerous hitters and finest second basemen of his era.

Morgan was born in Bonham, Texas, but grew up in Oakland, California. There, he played high school baseball and emulated his heroes—all players and second basemen—such as Jackie Robinson and Nellie Fox.

Major league scouts soon came around, and Morgan signed with the expansion Houston Colt .45s (the Astros after 1965) of the National League in 1963.

After one season in the minors, Morgan became Houston's second baseman in 1965. There, his coach ironically was Nellie Fox, who taught him a technique to "chicken flap" his elbow when he was at the plate in order to keep it high. Morgan responded by hitting .271, with 14 home runs and a league-leading 97 walks.

Morgan remained a solid player for Houston over the next several years, but despite his play, the team went nowhere in the standings. At the same time, the Cincinnati Reds were looking for an additional spark plug to add to their offense, and at the end of the 1971 season, Morgan was traded to the Reds for Tommy Helms.

The swap to Cincinnati was just what Morgan and the Reds needed. There, he became a vital cog in the "Big Red Machine," a team that, during the 1970s, won four National League pennants and back-to-back World Series titles in 1975 and 1976.

In those two world championship seasons, Morgan had the best years of his career. In 1975, he hit .327 with 17 homers, 94 RBIs, and 67 stolen bases. The following year, he slammed 27 homers to go with his 111 RBIs, 60 steals, and a .320 batting average. He won the league's Most Valuable Player (MVP) Award both years, becoming one of only a handful of players in baseball history to win the award consecutively.

Despite his relatively smaller size at only five foot seven and 150 pounds, Morgan was a powerful hitter in his prime, and he was just as likely to break up a ball game with a home run as he was with a single and a stolen base.

Morgan left the Reds after the 1979 season and finished his career playing one year or two with various clubs. After retiring in 1984, Morgan became a broadcaster, earning praise for both his insight and candor. He was elected to the Hall of Fame in 1990.

During the late 1960s, **TOM SEAVER** helped turn the New York Mets from the laughingstock of the National League into world champions—all in the span of two years.

The Mets knew they were getting someone special when they first signed him. Born in Fresno, California, George Thomas Seaver blossomed as a pitcher after playing under famed baseball coach Rod Dedeaux at the University of Southern California. Seaver was originally drafted by the Los Angeles Dodgers, with whom he refused to sign. He later signed with the Atlanta Braves for $40,000. However, because Seaver had already started another collegiate season, baseball Commissioner William D. Eckert voided the contract. Eckert ruled that every team had a shot at Seaver in a special lottery if they matched or topped the Braves' offer. Only three teams did, and they were the Phillies, the Indians, and the Mets.

Eckert then drew the Mets' name out of a hat, and they signed Seaver for $50,000

in 1966. Seaver went right into the big leagues the next season and showed that he belonged by posting a 16–13 record while the team finished in last place with a 61–101 win-loss record.

Then, in 1969, Seaver and his team shocked the baseball world. That year, the "Miracle Mets" won the pennant and then upset the heavily favored Baltimore Orioles to win the World Series. Seaver had become the staff ace with a record of 25–7, 208 strikeouts, and a 2.21 earned run average (ERA). He won the Cy Young Award as the league's best pitcher.

Seaver won the Cy Young Award twice more, in 1973 and 1975. In 1973, he again helped pitch the Mets to the pennant with a record of 19–10, 251 strikeouts, and a brilliant 2.08 ERA. That year, the Mets lost a tough seven-game World Series to the Oakland A's.

Although the Mets faltered in the standings during the mid-1970s, Seaver continued to pitch very well, leading the league in wins and strikeouts in 1975. In 1977, he was on his way to another fine season but became involved in a bitter contract dispute with the Mets' management. In the middle of the season, he was suddenly traded to Cincinnati. The deal sent the Mets into a downward spiral and was known as the "Wednesday Night Massacre."

Seaver had several fine seasons with Cincinnati, including a no-hitter in 1978, before finishing up his career in the American League in the 1980s. In 1985, he won his 300th game, and retired the following year with a winning percentage of .603 (311–205), the highest of any 300-game winner in fifty years. In 1992, he was elected to the Hall of Fame.

◆ The old saying, "Actions speak louder than words," could certainly apply to **STEVE CARLTON**. Throughout his entire twenty-four-year career, the left-hander who almost never spoke to the media let his pitching arm do the talking—to the tune of more than 300 wins, over 4,000 strikeouts, and four Cy Young Awards.

Steve Carlton was born in Miami, Florida, and was a three-sport star in high school. In 1964, he signed with the Cardinals, and in 1967, he broke into the St. Louis starting rotation when he went 14–9 with a 2.98 earned run average (ERA). The next year Carlton posted a 13–11 record with a 2.99 ERA. His pitching was part of the reason that St. Louis won the National League pennant both years. However, he was not a factor in either World Series, going 0–1 in 1967 and having no decisions in 1968.

It was in 1971, though, that Carlton emerged as one of the dominant hurlers in the league. He won 20 games while losing only 9, and it seemed as if he was the heir apparent to Bob Gibson as the staff's ace pitcher. However, he became embroiled in a salary dispute after that season and was traded to the Philadelphia Phillies.

In 1972, the Phillies were a last-place team and losers of 97 games, which makes what Carlton accomplished even more remarkable. The southpaw's victory total accounted for nearly half of the Phillies' wins. Carlton went 27–10 while leading the league in wins. He also led with a 1.97 ERA, 41 starts, 30 complete games, 346 innings pitched, and 310 strikeouts. He was an obvious choice for the Cy Young Award.

For the next thirteen years, Carlton was one of baseball's best pitchers. He won 20 games or more four more times, as well as three more Cy Young Awards in 1977, 1980, and 1982. In 1980, Carlton led Philadelphia to its first world championship in franchise history. He won 24 games in the regular season, one in the League Championship Series, and two more against the Kansas City Royals in the World Series.

Carlton's pitching repertoire featured a sharp-breaking slider that was almost impossible for right-handers to hit. A student of Eastern martial arts, Carlton adhered to a unique strength and conditioning program that included working his arm through a vat of rice. He was notoriously reclusive with the media and usually only spoke to them through his friend and favorite catcher, Tim McCarver.

He retired after the 1988 season with 329 victories as well as 4,136 strikeouts—second at the time only to Nolan Ryan. Carlton was elected to the Hall of Fame in 1994.

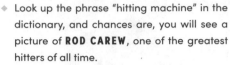

◆ Look up the phrase "hitting machine" in the dictionary, and chances are, you will see a picture of **ROD CAREW**, one of the greatest hitters of all time.

Carew was born in somewhat unique circumstances. His mother was a passenger on a train between the family home in Gatun and Panama City, Panama, when she gave birth to him in 1945. He didn't play baseball until he was fifteen years old, and at age seventeen, his family moved to New York City. It was here that a part-time scout for the Minnesota Twins spotted Carew belting out line drives.

Signed by the Twins, Carew spent three years in the minors, where he hit better than .300 twice. Promoted to the parent club in 1967, he hit .292 and won the American League's Rookie of the Year Award. Two years later, Carew won his first batting title by hitting .332. Carew owned the 1970s in terms of hitting in the league, winning six more batting titles, including four in a row

from 1972 to 1975. When his streak was interrupted in 1976 by George Brett's .333 average, Carew hit "only" .331.

Carew began his big league career as a second baseman, but he was moved to first base in 1977 to spare him from the relentless pounding that second basemen endure from sliding base runners. Carew responded to the switch by making the most serious run at a .400 average that the game had seen since Ted Williams last accomplished that number in 1941. He fell just short of that goal, hitting .388.

While Carew's skill with a bat was widely known, few people knew that he was an accomplished bunter. He would often put on a show for teammates and fans alike during batting practice by placing a handkerchief at various points up and down the first and third base foul lines and then bunting a ball directly into it.

Carew was also one of the premier base stealers in the league. Although he never led the circuit in steals, he was annually among the league leaders. In 1969, he stole home seven times, tying an existing record.

In 1979, Carew was traded to the California Angels and had several fine seasons with them.

Carew played in League Championship Series with both the Twins and Angels, but never enjoyed the thrill of participating in a World Series. However, in 1985 he did become only the sixteenth player in history to achieve 3,000 hits. He retired after that season, with a lifetime .328 average. He was elected to the Hall of Fame in 1991.

One of the great control pitchers of his era, **JIM "CATFISH" HUNTER** anchored the pitching staff of the three-time world champion Oakland A's team before joining the New York Yankees as a high-priced free agent in the mid-1970s.

Born in Hertford, North Carolina, James Augustus Hunter was a sensational schoolboy pitcher with a record of 26–2 and five no-hitters. The Kansas City A's, run by colorful owner Charlie O. Finley, signed Hunter right out of high school in 1964 for $75,000. To broaden his gate appeal, Finley gave Hunter the nickname "Catfish" because Hunter liked to hunt and fish.

Without ever pitching an inning in the minors, Hunter made his debut for the A's in 1965, posting an 8–8 mark. His lifetime record was an unremarkable 30–36 when the A's moved to Oakland in 1968. Hunter had hinted at the greatness to come, though, by throwing a perfect game against the Minnesota Twins early in the 1968 season.

Both Hunter and the A's blossomed in the West. The A's won three straight World Series from 1972 to 1974, and Hunter was the star of the pitching staff, winning 67 games and losing only 24 during those years. In 1974, he won the American League's Cy Young Award, leading the league in wins with 25. Throughout his time on the A's—a team filled with large egos who often battled among each other—the down-to-earth Hunter remained very popular with both teammates and fans alike.

When Finley failed to pay an insurance premium as contractually called for at the end of the 1974 season, an arbitrator ruled the contract as void. Hunter was then declared a free agent, and he sold his services to the highest bidder. The New York Yankees signed him for five years at $3.75 million, an unheard-of salary at the time.

Hunter won 23 games for the Yankees in 1975, making it the fifth straight year he had won more than 20. He won 17 the next year as the Yankees went to the World Series, but the team was swept by the Cincinnati Reds. Hunter then developed arm trouble and was only a shadow of his former self as the Yankees won back-to-back world championships in 1977 and 1978. After a 2–9 season in 1979, he retired at age thirty-three.

Over his lifetime, Hunter won 224 and lost just 166 games, and he posted a 3.26 earned run average (ERA). He also was at his best in big games. As a member of both the A's and Yankees, he won four League Championship Series games and another five World Series contests. He was elected to the Hall of Fame in 1987.

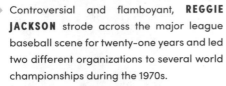

Controversial and flamboyant, **REGGIE JACKSON** strode across the major league baseball scene for twenty-one years and led two different organizations to several world championships during the 1970s.

Reginald Martinez Jackson was born in Wyncote, Pennsylvania, and started playing ball at an early age. Although he loved baseball, he excelled at football and went to Arizona State University on a football scholarship. While he was there, he found time to break the school baseball team's home run records. The Kansas City Athletics offered him an $85,000 bonus, and Jackson left college after his sophomore year.

He went up to the majors in 1967, and once the A's moved to Oakland in 1968, Jackson proved that he could be a star player. He hit 29 homers that year and 47 more in 1969. Then, beginning in 1970, led by Jackson and players such as Joe Rudi, Sal Bando, and Catfish Hunter, the team swept their way to five consecutive American

League Western Division titles, three pennants, and three consecutive world championships, from 1972 to 1974.

As the team's right fielder, Jackson's play was sometimes an adventure, but there was no denying his awesome power. In 1971, he hit a tremendous home run off the light tower in Detroit's Tiger Stadium during the All-Star Game, one of the longest homers ever hit in that ballpark. In 1973, he was the American League's Most Valuable Player (MVP) with a league leading 32 home runs and 117 RBIs.

Free agency broke up the A's after 1975, and Jackson wound up with the New York Yankees. There he fought with his teammates, including catcher Thurman Munson, manager Billy Martin, and owner George Steinbrenner, while leading the Yankees to two world championships in 1977 and 1978. In Game 6 of the 1977 World Series, Jackson hit three consecutive homers on three swings of the bat to win the world championship and earn the nickname "Mr. October." Babe Ruth was the only other player to hit three homers in one World Series game.

Proving that he was a winner wherever he went, Jackson joined the California Angels in 1982, sparking them to two Western Division titles in five years.

Jackson retired in 1987, with 563 home runs and 1,702 RBIs. In addition, his career World Series statistics were outstanding—a .357 average, 10 home runs, and 24 RBIs.

"There isn't enough mustard in all America to cover that hot dog," a teammate once said of Jackson, and it was true. However, while Jackson may have swaggered on the ball field, he backed it up with deeds. He was inducted into the Hall of Fame in 1993.

With his trademark black handlebar mustache, **ROLLIE FINGERS** looked like a riverboat gambler or the villain in a B-list movie—anything but one of the finest relief pitchers in baseball history.

Roland Glen Fingers was born in Steubenville, Ohio. After signing with the A's in his early twenties, he constantly switched between starting and coming out of the bullpen in the minor leagues. Brought up to the big league club in 1969, he was again bounced between both roles, having little success in either.

Finally, in 1971, Oakland A's manager Dick Williams took a hard look at Fingers's numbers and saw that, up to that time, he had only been able to finish 4 out of 35 starts in his career. At that moment, he decided to put Fingers permanently in the bullpen. The results were nothing short of remarkable. Fingers saved 17 games for the A's that season and 21 games in 1972. The A's suddenly realized that they had found one of the premier relievers in the game.

Fingers was a vital part of the A's drive to their three straight world championships beginning in 1972. Fingers saved 61 games during those years, and frequently rescued a struggling starter even when he didn't receive credit for a save. Fingers proved how valuable he was, particularly in the 1974 World Series. He won one game and saved two others, winning Most Valuable Player (MVP) for the Series as the A's beat the Los Angeles Dodgers in five games.

Tall and lanky, Fingers had a distinctive look on the mound that was only enhanced by his facial hair. During his tenure with the team, owner Charles O. Finley had his players all grow mustaches as part of a promotional gimmick. Fingers grew a sweeping handlebar mustache that became his trademark.

After the 1976 season, Fingers left the A's and joined the San Diego Padres in the National League, becoming one of the early groups of free agents in pro baseball. In each of his first two seasons with San Diego, Fingers led the league in saves. In 1978, he saved 37 games, which became the most in his career.

Perhaps his finest season came in 1981, after he was traded back to the American League and joined the Milwaukee Brewers. That year, Fingers saved 28 games and posted a brilliant 1.04 earned run average (ERA). His stellar pitching performance won him both the MVP Award and the Cy Young Award as the league's best pitcher.

Elbow problems hampered Fingers in later years, and he retired after the 1985 season. When he quit, he had saved a total of 341 games—the most in major league history at that time. He was elected to the Hall of Fame in 1992.

The most overpowering pitcher of his generation, **NOLAN RYAN** won more than 300 games, struck out a record-breaking 5,714 batters, and threw an incredible seven no-hitters during a major league career that stretched across four decades.

Ryan was born in Refugio, Texas, and grew up in Alvin, Texas. Drafted by the New York Mets in 1965, he signed for a $30,000 bonus, and went up to the majors for good in 1968. Even though Ryan showed flashes of brilliance, his four seasons with the Mets could only be described as mediocre. His record was 29–37, and he was constantly wild, averaging six walks per nine innings.

Thinking that Ryan would never realize his potential, the Mets traded him to the California Angels of the American League for third baseman Jim Fregosi after the 1971 season. It is often considered one of the worst trades in baseball history.

With the Angels, Ryan blossomed into a superstar. He won 19, 21, and 22 games

his first three years with the team and led the American League in strikeouts during all three seasons. In 1973, he struck out an astounding 383 batters, breaking the record set by Sandy Koufax in 1965. In his career, Ryan struck out more than 300 batters in a season six times—a major league record.

Ryan was literally unhittable at times. In 1973, he pitched his first two no-hitters just two months apart. In the second one, against the Detroit Tigers, first baseman Norm Cash felt so overmatched that he went up to bat with a table leg. Ryan would go on to throw five more career no-hitters, which tallied three more than anyone else in history. The last one came in 1991 when he was forty-four years old.

In 1979, Ryan left the Angels and signed a free agent contract with the Houston Astros to be closer to his family in Texas. He also became baseball's first pro player to earn $1 million a year. He moved to the Texas Rangers in 1989 and ended his career with them.

Ryan threw as hard as any pitcher in history, his fastball often exceeding 100 miles per hour. Even at the end of his career, "the Ryan Express" was timed consistently at over 90 miles per hour.

Unfortunately, Ryan didn't get to play on many winning teams. He was in one World Series in 1969 with the Mets and a few League Championship Series with the Angels and Astros. While he barely won more games than he lost in his career with 324–292, his record is more of an indictment of the poor teams that he played on than a reflection of his pitching ability.

Nolan Ryan was inducted into the Hall of Fame in 1999.

Many say that **JOHNNY BENCH** was the best all-around catcher in the history of professional baseball.

Bench was born in Oklahoma City, Oklahoma, and grew up admiring Mickey Mantle, another great Oklahoman. Like his hero, Bench was an outstanding ballplayer as a youngster, and he was drafted by the Cincinnati Reds in 1965.

After two good years with the Reds' Tampa Bay minor league club, Bench burst onto the big league scene with in 1968. He hit .275 with 15 homers and 82 RBIs and won the National League's Rookie of the Year Award.

But Bench was just getting warmed up. In 1970, he won the league's Most Valuable Player (MVP) Award, hitting .293 and leading the league with 45 homers and 148 RBIs. At age twenty-two, he became the youngest player ever to win the award. Two years later he won MVP again, hitting .270 with 40 homers and 125 RBIs.

Bench also helped lead Cincinnati to the National League playoffs and the World Series during those two years. The Reds were gradually forming what would become one of the most dominant teams in baseball, known as the "Big Red Machine." Along with players like Pete Rose, Joe Morgan, and Tony Perez, Bench was a key member of that team.

In 1975, the Reds beat the Boston Red Sox in a memorable seven-game World Series, and the following year, Cincinnati wiped out the New York Yankees 4–0 in the Series. Although Bench hit poorly in the 1975 Series, he bounced back to hit an outstanding .533 with two homers and six RBIs in the 1976 contest. Asked to compare Bench's play to that of Yankees catcher Thurman Munson, who had just hit .529, Reds manager Sparky Anderson said, "I don't want to embarrass any other catcher by comparing him to Johnny Bench."

Although the remark angered Munson and his many fans, it was true: Bench was the predominant catcher in the game, both offensively and defensively. Behind the plate, he popularized a one-handed style of catching, which gave him the opportunity to throw more efficiently. Soon an entire generation of youngsters were imitating Bench's method, much to the dismay of their coaches.

Bench had a rocket-throwing arm and was as nimble as a cat behind the plate. Base runners became so intimidated by his success at throwing them out that many of them simply stopped running on him. Bench won ten Gold Glove Awards in his career.

Bench spent his entire seventeen-year career with the Reds. He was voted into the Hall of Fame in 1989.

After **MIKE SCHMIDT**'s first full season in the majors, few would have predicted that he would be called the best third baseman in baseball history by the time he retired.

Born and raised in Dayton, Ohio, Schmidt damaged his knees playing football as a youngster. Consequently, he attracted little interest from baseball scouts. Schmidt went to Ohio University, where his exceptional play for the college team convinced the Philadelphia Phillies to take a chance on him. They signed him for $32,500 and a series of $2,500 bonuses. It turned out to be the best money the Phillies ever spent.

Schmidt became the club's regular third baseman in 1973, and while he hit 18 homers, his other numbers were dismal: he batted .196 and struck out 136 times. However, the following year he raised his average nearly 100 points to .282, hit a league-leading 36 homers, and helped Philadelphia climb to a third-place finish—the team's best results in ten years.

By 1978, the Phillies, led by Schmidt and others, including Steve Carlton and Larry Bowa, had become one of the best teams in the majors. They won their third straight National League Eastern Division title, though they lost the pennant each time. Schmidt had also become one of the most feared power hitters in the game and led the league in homers for the third straight year with 38. In 1976, he had become one of only a handful of players to hit four home runs in one game.

The Phillies finally won the pennant in 1980 and then went on to win their first world championship, beating the Kansas City Royals in six games in the World Series. Schmidt had a career-high 48 homers and 121 RBIs during that season and was named the league's Most Valuable Player (MVP). He continued his hot hitting during the World Series, batting .381 with two homers and seven RBIs and was named the Series MVP. Schmidt won two more league MVP Awards in 1981 and 1986.

Schmidt was more than just a devastating hitter. Although he was not known for his defensive skills when he first went up, he turned himself into one of the best fielding third basemen in history. He won a whopping ten Gold Glove Awards during his career.

Schmidt retired with 548 lifetime home runs—the most for any third baseman, and at the time, seventh on the all-time list. He led the National League in home runs eight times and drove in at least 100 runs nine times. He was elected to the Hall of Fame in 1995.

A slashing line-drive hitter with surprising power, **GEORGE BRETT** was perhaps the best-hitting third baseman in American League history.

Brett was born in Glen Dale, West Virginia, to a baseball-loving family. His older brother Ken became the youngest player ever to pitch in a World Series game when he appeared in the 1967 Series with the Boston Red Sox at the age of nineteen.

After high school, George attended El Camino College in Torrance, California. However, when the Kansas City Royals of the American League came calling in 1971, George decided that he wanted to follow his brother Ken and pursue a baseball career.

After signing with the Royals, Brett played a few years in the minors, giving no indication that he was a hitting machine or a budding superstar. When he took over as the team's regular third baseman in mid-1974, he batted a rather ordinary .282.

However, around that time, Brett was coming under the influence of Royals' coach Charlie Lau and his hitting theories. The theories must have paid off immediately for Brett, for the next season, he hit .308, then followed that up with a .333 average in 1976, which was good enough for the American League batting title. He hit .300 or better in seven out of the next nine years.

Brett's ultimate hitting season came in 1980, when he seriously challenged Ted Williams's legendary .400 mark. Most baseball observers feel that hitting .400 is virtually impossible for the modern player because of the extensive travel required of players and the rise of the late inning relief specialist. Brett came as close as any player ever has to cracking the magical barrier since Williams last did it in 1941, recording over .400 as late as the first week of September and then tailing off to finish at .390. That season, he also hit 24 home runs and knocked in 118 runs to lead the Royals to their first pennant. He was also voted the league's Most Valuable Player (MVP).

During his career, Brett became one of the most feared hitters in the American League, a singles and doubles hitter who still averaged between 15–20 home runs each year. When he hit .329 in 1990 to win his third batting title, he became the first player to ever lead the American League in hitting in three separate decades.

Led by Brett, the Royals won several titles in the division, two pennants, and the world championship in 1985.

Brett spent his entire career with the Royals and retired after the 1993 season with a .305 lifetime batting average and 3,154 hits. He was voted into the Hall of Fame in 1999.

RICKEY HENDERSON is baseball's stolen base king, both for career and for a single season, and he is probably the greatest leadoff hitter in baseball history.

Henderson was born in Chicago, Illinois, and grew up in Oakland, California. He was a star player in high school in both football and baseball, and the Oakland A's drafted and signed him for $10,000.

Henderson credits Tom Trebelhorn, who managed him in the minors and later skippered the Milwaukee Brewers, with teaching him how to steal bases. Henderson had always had the blazing speed, but Trebelhorn taught him how to study the pitcher and pick up subtle signals that reveal whether a pitcher is going to go home or throw to first.

Proving himself to be a quick study, Henderson stole 95 bases in his first full year in the minors in 1977. He also tied a record by stealing seven bases in one game.

In 1979, his first year with the big club,

Henderson stole only 33 bases. However, in 1980, Henderson swiped 100 bases and had a .303 batting average.

Then, in 1982, Henderson stole 130 bases to break Lou Brock's record of 118 steals in a single season—a record that was set just eight years prior. Ironically, Brock himself had tutored Henderson on the finer points of base stealing just that winter.

From that point on, Henderson became baseball's most dreaded base bandit. During the 1980s, he led the American League in steals nine times. Finally, in 1991, Henderson broke another Brock record of most lifetime stolen bases with 939. Throughout the 1990s, Henderson continued to swipe bases at a tremendous pace, averaging nearly 50 steals each year. By the end of the 2002 season, his total had reached 1,403. With the stolen base play declining as an offensive threat, Henderson's records may well remain unbroken forever.

Not only could Henderson steal bases, but he could hit with power. In 2001, he became the twenty-fifth player in history to accumulate 3,000 hits. During his career, Henderson also had nearly 300 homers, with many from the leadoff position. In fact, his capacity to turn a walk or a single into a double, combined with his power, make him the greatest leadoff threat of all-time.

Despite his success, Henderson remained a controversial player throughout his career. Outspoken and often self-absorbed, he wore out his welcome on every club with which he played. By the end of 2002, he had been with eight different teams—an incredible number for such a star player. He officially retired in 2007 and was inducted into the Hall of Fame in 2009.

When he stepped up to the plate, **TONY GWYNN** might not have looked like a classic hitter. He was neither tall and lean like Ted Williams nor smooth and graceful like Joe DiMaggio. However, when Gwynn swung, spraying the ball with authority on all fields, he obliterated any doubts that he was one the best pure hitters in baseball history.

Gwynn was born in Los Angeles, California, and grew up in San Diego. In school, he excelled in both baseball and basketball. In fact, in 1981—the same year that the baseball's San Diego Padres drafted him—Gwynn was selected by the San Diego Clippers of the National Basketball Association (NBA).

However, it was baseball that was in Gwynn's blood, and he signed with the Padres. While Gwynn showed immediate promise as a hitter, injuries slowed him in both 1982 and 1983. Even so, playing in only 86 games in 1983, he hit .309.

The following year, Gwynn regained his health, and he blistered the ball at a .351 clip, winning the National League batting title. However, Gwynn was just getting started. After "slumping" to batting averages of .317 and .329 in 1985 and 1986, respectively, Gwynn hit .370 in 1987 to win his second batting crown. It was also the first of three consecutive years that Gwynn would be the league batting champ. He won the title again the following year with a .313 average and took the crown once more that following year with a .336 mark.

Gwynn's heavy hitting helped the Padres reach the World Series twice during his career—in 1984 and 1998. Although the Padres lost both times, Gwynn's batting average for the nine games that he played in was .371. Against the New York Yankees in 1998, Gwynn hit .500 for the Series while the Yankees swept the Padres for four games straight.

Gwynn led the National League in batting eight times during his twenty-year career. A line drive and singles hitter who seemingly never gets fooled at the plate, Gwynn also holds the league record for attaining five or more hits in one game, which he did four times. Even during the last few years of his career, when injuries seriously hampered his performance, Gwynn continued to sting the ball, hitting over .300 in both 2000 and 2001.

Gwynn retired at the end of the 2001 season with a sparkling lifetime batting average of .338 and 3,141 hits. A well-liked player throughout his career, he was an articulate spokesman for the game, and after his retirement, he began working in sports broadcasting. He was inducted into the Hall of Fame in 2007.

CAL RIPKEN JR. broke the one baseball record widely considered untouchable: Lou Gehrig's mark of 2,130 consecutive games played. The tall, rangy Ripken also redefined the shortstop position, bringing power to a spot traditionally occupied by singles hitters, showing that a big man could play the position with skill and grace.

Ripken had his sights set on becoming a pro baseball player ever since childhood in Havre de Grace, Maryland. It seems only natural that baseball was in his blood since his father, Cal Sr., played and managed in the Baltimore Orioles system, and his mother was a standout softball player in high school.

In high school, Ripken was a good shortstop and an even better pitcher. In his senior year, he struck out 100 batters in 60 innings. Even though several teams were interested in him, Ripken only wanted to play for the Baltimore Orioles. At six foot four, Ripken did not fit the traditional mold of a shortstop, but he played both shortstop and third base in the Orioles minor league system.

Promoted to the majors in 1982, Ripken entered the American League with a bang as shortstop. He hit .264 with 28 homers and 93 RBIs—totals that won him the Rookie of the Year Award. On May 29, 1982, Ripken sat out for one game. It would be the last game he would miss for the next sixteen years. The next day, he began his remarkable run at Gehrig's record.

The following year, Ripken hit .318 with 27 homers, 47 doubles, and 102 RBIs. He helped lead the Orioles to a World Series triumph over the Philadelphia Phillies and was voted the American League's Most Valuable Player (MVP). He won another MVP Award in 1991.

Meanwhile, he continued his amazing streak of playing in every game. On the night of September 6, 1995, Ripken broke Gehrig's record by playing in his 2,131st consecutive game. Many people believe that Ripken's run for Gehrig's record, and the classy manner with which he conducted himself during the challenge, brought fans back to baseball who had been alienated by the 1994 players' strike and World Series cancellation. Overall, Ripken played in 2,632 straight games, voluntarily ending the streak on September 20, 1998.

At the conclusion of the 2001 season, Ripken retired. He hit the most homers by a shortstop in baseball history with 345, was one of just seven players to have 3,000 hits and 400 homers, and set a record by playing 8,243 consecutive innings. The man once thought of as too big to play shortstop ended his career as one of the greatest shortstops in baseball history. He was elected to the Hall of Fame in 2007.

◆ Known early in his career for his temper as much as his blazing fastball, **ROGER CLEMENS** defied the experts who said he would never have a lengthy career because he would either blow out his arm or permanently "blow up" on the mound.

Although he was born in Dayton, Ohio, Clemens is most often associated with Texas. His family moved there when he was fourteen, and he first gained national attention when he helped lead the University of baseball team to the 1983 NCAA championship. After college, he was drafted and signed by the Boston Red Sox.

Clemens went up to the Red Sox in 1984, and his first two seasons were mediocre. Then, in 1986, he dominated the American League, posting a record of 24–4, with a 2.48 earned run average (ERA) and 238 strikeouts. That year, he won his first Cy Young Award. The next season, Clemens was 20–9 with 256 strikeouts and a 2.97 ERA when he won his second Cy Young Award and clearly established himself as one of the best young pitchers in baseball.

Clemens continued to be the ace of Boston's pitching staff throughout the early and mid-1990s. However, the team never won the World Series during his time, although they finished within one out in 1986. In addition, Clemens had become known for being somewhat volatile, especially in big games, when he would get so worked up that it would hurt his effectiveness. In one notorious incident, he became so enraged with the home plate umpire in a pivotal American League championship contest that he got thrown out of the game in the second inning.

Clemens left Boston in a bitter dispute with management in 1997, and he moved to the Toronto Blue Jays. He had two brilliant years there in 1997 and 1998 and won two more Cy Young Awards.

However, the thrill of winning a World Series still eluded Clemens. Thus, he hoped that a trade to the New York Yankees in 1999 would finally gain him a championship ring. The Yankees did indeed win the World Series in 1999 and 2000, with Clemens contributing victories in both the playoffs and the Series.

In 2001, Clemens defied those who said that his career would begin to decline as he neared forty. He became the first pitcher ever to start a season 20–1 en route to a record of 20–3, 213 strikeouts, and an unprecedented sixth Cy Young Award.

In 2003, using the same blazing fastball he had thrown at the beginning of his career, Clemens achieved his 300th win and his 4,000th strikeout in the same game. Unfortunately, his success around this time was called into question when he was accused of using performance-enhancing drugs as part of professional baseball's steroid scandal. Clemens continually denied that he had ever used steroids and pitched his last major league game in 2007.

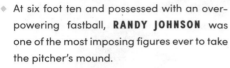

◆ At six foot ten and possessed with an overpowering fastball, **RANDY JOHNSON** was one of the most imposing figures ever to take the pitcher's mound.

Born in Walnut Creek, California, Johnson was already over six feet tall by the time he was in sixth grade. He struck out 121 batters in just 66 innings in his senior year of high school, and major league scouts were beating down his door. However, he decided to attend the University of Southern California, where he continued to display major league potential. The Montreal Expos drafted and signed him in 1985.

Johnson spent a few years in the minors honing his skills, particularly his control. However, he still had a reputation for wildness when he went up to the majors.

Johnson appeared in a few games with Montreal in 1988, and then early in the following season, he was traded to the Seattle Mariners of the American League. There, Johnson blossomed as a great pitcher. In

1990, he won 14 games and threw a no-hitter. In 1994, he almost certainly would have won 20 games if the players' strike in August hadn't wiped out the remainder of the season. He finished with a record of 19–8 with a 3.24 earned run average (ERA).

The following season, Johnson posted an 18–2 record with a 2.48 ERA and 248 strikeouts. He also pitched the Mariners into the postseason and won his first Cy Young Award.

In 1997, Johnson won 20 games for the first time and set an American League record for left-handers with 19 strikeouts in one game. After signing a $52 million deal with the Arizona Diamondbacks of the National League in November 1998, Johnson posted marks of 17–9 and 19–7 over the next two seasons to win two more Cy Young Awards. In the 2000 season, he struck out 347 batters.

In 2001, "The Big Unit" had a 21–6 record, and he combined with Curt Schilling to form a devastating one-two pitching punch to lead the Diamondbacks to the World Series for the first time.

In the team's victory over the New York Yankees, Johnson won three games—including a victory in relief in the deciding seventh game—to join a select group of pitchers who have won three games in one World Series. That year, Johnson won his third straight Cy Young Award, making it the fourth in his career.

Johnson had another dominating season in 2002. He was 24–5, with a 2.32 ERA and 334 strikeouts, winning the pitching Triple Crown as he won his fourth consecutive Cy Young Award (fifth total). Even after turning forty, the imposing left-hander hardly slowed down. He completed stints with the Yankees, the Diamondbacks, and the San Francisco Giants before retiring in 2009. He was elected to the Hall of Fame in 2015.

In 1998, **MARK MCGWIRE** broke the most celebrated record in baseball—61 home runs in a single season—and his pursuit of the cherished mark electrified fans all across the country.

McGwire was born in 1963, in Pomona, California. His baseball career was foreshadowed by his first time at bat in Little League when he was ten years old and hit a home run.

McGwire was drafted out of high school by the Montreal Expos but decided to attend the University of Southern California instead. After he played for the 1984 U.S. Olympic team, he was drafted and signed by the Oakland A's, who gave him a $150,000 bonus.

McGwire went up to the A's as a full-time player in 1987 and proved that he belonged in the majors immediately by smashing 49 homers—a rookie record.

The A's were rebuilding. Another powerful young slugger named Jose Canseco and McGwire were nicknamed the "Bash Brothers" for their ability to hit home runs and club opposing teams into submission. Along with other star players, including pitchers Dave Stewart and Dennis Eckersley, the A's won three straight American League pennants from 1988 to 1990. Oakland won the earthquake-interrupted World Series in 1989 by sweeping their Bay Area rivals, the San Francisco Giants.

The A's declined during the 1990s, but McGwire continued to pound the ball. In 1990, he became the first player to hit more than 30 home runs in his first four seasons. In 1992, he hit 42 homers, then followed that up with 52 in 1996. He then hit the astounding total of 58 homers in 1997, in a season split between the A's and the St. Louis Cardinals, to whom he'd been traded. It was the most home runs hit since Roger Maris's 61 in 1961.

As it turned out, McGwire's sensational 1997 season was only a preview of what would happen in 1998. All summer long, "Big Mac" and Chicago Cubs slugger Sammy Sosa (see no. 98) captivated the nation as they dueled for the home run crown, both players clearly having a shot at Maris's record.

Finally, on September 8, 1998, McGwire hit his 62nd home run, eclipsing Maris's mark. Through his friendly rivalry with Sosa, and his gracious manner, McGwire won back the hearts of many baseball fans who had been embittered by the disastrous 1994 players' strike. McGwire finished the year with 70 homers over Sosa's 66.

The following year, McGwire hit 65 home runs, but it was to be his last hurrah. Bothered by chronic injuries, he retired after the 2001 season with 583 lifetime homers, which at the time ranked fifth overall on the career home run list.

Unfortunately, many of McGwire's career successes were dampened when he admitted in 2010 to using steroids on and off throughout the 1990s to aid in his recovery from injuries. Despite this, he is still considered by many to be one of baseball's best players.

Voted player of the decade in the nineties, **BARRY BONDS** spent the early years of the following decade rewriting baseball's record book in unprecedented ways.

In 2001, the slugging left-handed outfielder smashed 73 homers to break the single-season record set by Mark McGwire just three years prior. Bonds also hit .328, drove in 137 runs, and set a new single-season slugging percentage of .863, breaking Babe Ruth's eighty-two-year-old mark of .847. And he accomplished all this while National League pitchers walked him a record 177 times to break another Ruth record.

A native of Riverside, California, Bonds was born to be a ballplayer— his father is Bobby Bonds, who combined speed and power as a star player for several teams during the 1970s and 1980s, and his godfather is Willie Mays, the legendary Giants outfielder.

Bonds spent the first seven years of his career with the Pittsburgh Pirates. In that time, he led the team to three straight Eastern Division titles, and in 1990 and 1992, he was named the National League's Most Valuable Player (MVP). However, the Pirates failed to advance to the World Series each year, and in 1993, Bonds accepted a large free agent contract to play for the San Francisco Giants.

In his first season with the Giants, Bonds hit .336 with 46 home runs and 123 RBIs. For the third time in four years, he was named the league MVP. Bonds continued to put up great numbers for the Giants throughout the

nineties and helped lead the team to two Western Division titles. Yet an appearance in the World Series remained an elusive goal as the Giants failed to advance in the playoffs.

After his record-shattering 2001 season, for which he won an unprecedented fourth MVP Award, Bonds kept right on going. The next year, he won his first batting title with a .370 batting average, broke his own record for walks with 198, and hit 46 home runs. Bonds also joined Willie Mays, Babe Ruth, and Hank Aaron as the only players to have 600 or more career home runs. He won his fifth MVP and led the Giants to their first pennant in thirteen years.

In the National League playoffs, Bonds was outstanding. Then, in a dramatic World Series against the California Angels, he hit .471 with 4 home runs and 6 RBIs. Though the Giants ultimately lost in seven games, Bonds had demolished the longtime knock on his reputation that he couldn't deliver in the clutch in the postseason.

Bonds seemed to only get better with age, with perhaps his best season coming in 2004, the year he turned forty. He walked 232 times, breaking his own record, batted .362, and slugged .812—the fourth highest of all time. Unfortunately, much of his later success was cast into doubt by his alleged involvement in baseball's 2003 steroid scandal, when his trainer was charged with supplying performance-enhancing drugs to athletes. Bonds played his last major league game in 2007, and despite the controversy, is still widely considered one of the greatest baseball players of all time.

There are pitchers who win because they have dominating skills like a blazing fastball or a sharp breaking curve ball. Then there are pitchers who win because they are control artists, moving the ball around and painting the corners of the plate. **GREG MADDUX**, one of the best pitchers in the game in the nineties, falls into the second category.

Maddux was born in San Angelo, Texas, but his father was in the U.S. Air Force, so the family moved around regularly. The one constant in Greg Maddux's life was baseball. No matter where he was living, Maddux found a baseball diamond, or he practiced in the backyard with his father. The result was that he developed many remarkable skills early, such as a smooth pitching motion and pinpoint accuracy.

Despite his small size at five foot eleven and 150 pounds, Maddux was considered such an accomplished pitcher when he graduated high school that the Chicago Cubs signed him with an $85,000 bonus in 1984. After some impressive minor league pitching, he was called up to the Cubs late in the 1986 season.

After suffering through a poor season in 1987, Maddux came into his own in 1988. He won 18 games and posted a 3.18 earned run average (ERA). That began a remarkable string for him across fourteen straight seasons from 1988 to 2001, in which Maddux did not win less than 15 games or pitch less than 200 innings.

In 1992 and 1993, Maddux reeled off back-to-back 20-win seasons. In 1994 and 1995, he posted ERAs of 1.56 and 1.63, becoming the first pitcher since Walter Johnson to have two consecutive seasons with an ERA under 1.80. Maddux accomplished all this with just an average fastball. He rarely ever threw above 90 miles per hour but had an uncanny command of a variety of pitches, which he placed in precise spots to frustrate batters.

Maddux also won four consecutive National League Cy Young Awards from 1992 to 1995 as the league's best pitcher—a feat never accomplished before. An excellent fielder, he won Gold Glove Awards as the league's best fielding pitcher every year during the 1990s.

Maddux joined the Atlanta Braves as a free agent prior to the 1993 season and combined with Tom Glavine and John Smoltz to form a "Big Three" that was one of the most dominant trios in recent memory. They helped Atlanta consistently get to the postseason and win the World Series in 1995.

Greg Maddux remained one of the best pitchers in baseball as he entered the 2000s. He joined the ranks of baseball's immortals in 2004 when he returned to the Cubs and reached 300 career wins. In 2005, he achieved his 3,000th strikeout. He retired in 2008 after he was awarded his eighteenth Gold Glove Award.

SAMMY SOSA is one of those rare players who doesn't seem initially destined for greatness but suddenly matures into a bona fide superstar.

For certain, there was no hint of stardom in Sosa's early life and baseball career. Born in San Pedro de Macoris in the Dominican Republic, Sosa was only seven years old when his father died. As a youngster, Sosa had to do whatever he could to help support the family, including shining shoes, selling oranges, and washing cars.

Sosa did not play in his first baseball game until he was fourteen years old. Nevertheless, his natural ability got him into a baseball camp run by the Toronto Blue Jays in Santo Domingo. It was there that he was spotted by a scout for the Texas Rangers, who signed him for a $3,500 bonus.

Sosa showed little promise with the Rangers, though, and in mid-1989, he was traded to the Chicago White Sox. Despite showing flashes of brilliance with the White Sox, before the start of the 1992 season, Sosa was traded again—this time across town to the Chicago Cubs.

Working with former Cubs Hall of Famer Billy Williams, Sosa began to mature as a hitter. In 1993, he became the first "30–30" player in Cubs history, hitting 33 homers and stealing 36 bases. In the strike-interrupted year that followed, Sosa hit 25 homers, then followed that up with seasons of 36, 40, and 36 home runs. He had become one of the National League's premier sluggers.

Still, nobody was prepared for what happened in 1998. As a captivated country watched, Sosa dueled with Mark McGwire for the major league home run crown throughout the entire season, as each one challenged the magic mark of 61 that had been set thirty-seven years earlier by Roger Maris. When the dust had settled, McGwire emerged as the winner, belting 70 homers over Sosa's 66. Although McGwire won the home run derby, Sosa also became popular with fans everywhere for the enthusiasm he displayed every time he took to the field. He also earned Most Valuable Player (MVP) honors as he led the Cubs to their first playoff appearance in nine years.

Proving that the 1998 season was no fluke, Sosa hit 63 homers in 1999. In 2001, he belted 64 homers with 160 RBIs, but his superlative season was overshadowed by Barry Bonds' successful quest to break McGwire's record.

After another fine season in 2002, Sosa began 2003 by entering the record books. In early April, he became the eighteenth player in history to hit 500 career home runs. However, his successes around this time were overshadowed by accusations that he had been involved in baseball's 2003 steroid scandal, though he denied ever using illegal performance-enhancing drugs. After leaving the Cubs in 2004 and completing short stints with the Baltimore Orioles and the Texas Rangers, Sosa announced his retirement in 2009, stating that he would "calmly wait" for his induction into the Hall of Fame.

Tagged as a "superstar" when he was barely past his teens, **KEN GRIFFEY JR.** spent much of his career living up to that lofty title.

Given his baseball pedigree, it's not hard to imagine why "Junior" Griffey became an exceptional player. His father is Ken Griffey, who was an excellent player during his seventeen-year career, most notably with the Cincinnati Reds "Big Red Machine" of the 1970s.

Born in Donora, Pennsylvania, Junior showed his own talent early. He was such a great high school player that there were often more scouts than fans in the bleachers to watch his games. The Seattle Mariners made him their number one draft pick in 1987.

He spent portions of two seasons in the minors, but after a red-hot spring training in 1989, the Mariners made the nineteen-year-old rookie their starting center fielder. Griffey proved that they made the right decision by hitting .264 in his first season, with 16 homers and 61 RBIs.

The following season, both Griffeys made baseball history when Ken Sr. joined the Mariners, and they became the first father-and-son combination ever to play on the same team at the same time. Junior responded to his father's presence by cranking up his batting totals to .300, 22 homers, and 80 RBIs. In 1991, Junior raised his batting average even higher to. 327, and drove in 100 runs. He was now recognized as one of the best young players in the majors.

In 1993, Junior attached the "slugger" label firmly to himself when he blasted 45 home runs. From that point on, Griffey hit 40 or more homers for six out of the next seven seasons, with his peak coming in 1997 and 1998, when he hit 56 each year.

Griffey's defensive play got as many rave reviews as his hitting. He frequently scaled outfield fences to rob batters of extra base hits and home runs. During his career with Seattle, he won a Gold Glove Award ten times.

In 2000, the low-budget Mariners felt they could not afford to re-sign Griffey, who was soon to be eligible for free agency. So prior to the season, they traded him to the Cincinnati Reds. For Griffey, it was fulfilling his lifelong dream of playing on the team on which his father had once starred.

Griffey hit his 600th lifetime home run on June 9, 2008, and shortly afterward, he was traded to the Chicago White Sox. He returned to the Mariners in 2009, and in April, he hit his 400th home run as a Mariner. He retired in 2010 and was inducted into the Hall of Fame in 2016 as one of the greatest home run hitters in baseball history.

Many players, including some great Hall of Famers who had long careers, were never fortunate enough to win or even play in a World Series. After **DEREK JETER** had been in the majors for six seasons, he had already played in five World Series—and had four championship rings to show for it.

Born in New Jersey, Jeter already had his sights set on playing shortstop for the New York Yankees when he was a young boy. The Yankees drafted him after an outstanding high school career and signed him with an $800,000 bonus. Jeter raced through their minor league system, and at the tender age of twenty-one, he found himself starting at shortstop for the Yankees at the beginning of the 1996 season.

He hit .314 with 10 homers and 78 RBIs, winning the American League's Rookie of the Year Award. His solid play was a big reason that the Yankees won the pennant and then beat the Atlanta Braves in the World Series.

In 1998, both Jeter and the Yankees stood the rest of the league up on its ear. The team

won 114 games, setting a new American League record. The Yankees then roared through the playoffs before sweeping the San Diego Padres in the World Series. For his part, Jeter hit .324, with 19 homers and 84 RBIs. He also displayed significant speed, stealing 30 bases while only getting caught six times.

The following year, Jeter continued his hot hitting. He set career marks with his .349 batting average, 24 home runs, and 102 RBIs. His all-around sterling play was key to the Yankees sweeping the World Series again, this time against the Atlanta Braves.

Even though Jeter dipped in his batting categories a bit in the 2000 season with a .339 average, 15 homers, and 73 RBIs, the Yankees again won the World Series. This time, they dispatched their cross-town rivals, the New York Mets, in five games. While the Yankees lost the 2001 Series to the Arizona Diamondbacks, Jeter had another great season, hitting .311 with 21 home runs.

Jeter ended 2002 with a .317 career batting average, 117 homers, and 167 stolen bases. After only seven seasons, he had not only become one of the most popular Yankees, but to many, he was also the unofficial team captain. From the key infield shortstop position, his natural talent and baseball savviness seemed to be the glue that held the formidable team together.

Jeter ended up being a "career pinstriper," playing his entire twenty-year major league baseball career with the Yankees, helping them win five World Series. He served as team captain from 2003 until his retirement in 2014. He finished his career with 3,465 hits, five Gold Glove Awards, and five Silver Slugger Awards. He was inducted into the Hall of Fame in 2020, his first year of eligibility, only one vote shy of a unanimous selection.

TRIVIA QUESTIONS

Test your knowledge and challenge your friends with the following questions. The answers are contained in the biographies noted.

1. Which Hall of Fame shortstop's baseball card sold for over $450,000 nearly seventy years after he retired? (See no. 5)

2. Who said that the secret to managing is "to keep the guys who hate you away from the guys who are undecided"? (See no. 16)

3. How did one of baseball's best pitchers become the greatest slugger and home run hitter of his era? (See no. 18)

4. When did one of the National League's best pitchers strike out five of the American League's greatest hitters in a row? (See no. 29)

5. Which famous Yankee pitcher claimed he owed all his success to "clean living and a fast outfield"? (See no. 38)

6. How did the actions of a Brooklyn Dodger shortstop help pave the way for Jackie Robinson's acceptance into major league baseball? (See no. 45)

7. Why was the career of one Hall-of-Fame catcher cut tragically short? (See no. 50)

8. Where did baseball's first real relief specialist learn about the unique pitch that would make him famous? (See no. 53)

9. Which great superstar succeeded another legendary superstar by playing on the same team and in the same position? (See no. 59)

10. When did a Giants' Hall-of-Fame outfielder make what is considered the greatest catch in baseball history? (See no. 61)

11. Who gave some simple advice that helped turn a struggling, average pitcher into a brilliant Hall of Famer? (See no. 70)

12. Which pitcher won more games in the 1960s than anyone else but was often overshadowed by two other dominant pitchers of his era? (See no. 74)

13. Why was a star pitcher for the Oakland A's during the 1970s declared a free agent by a baseball arbitrator? (See no. 83)

14. Who became baseball's first player to earn $1 million annually in 1979? (See no. 86)

15. Where did the first player to ever lead the American League in hitting in three separate decades spend his entire career? (See no. 89)

16. Which player joined his own godfather on the list of the only players to have hit 600 or more career home runs? (See no. 96)

PROJECT SUGGESTIONS

1. Choose one of the baseball players from this book and write a one-page fictional diary entry for one day in that person's life. Pick a day that had some significance for the individual. For example: the day he had a great performance in a game, was inducted into the Hall of Fame, or achieved some other noteworthy success. Or choose a day on which the person was met with a personal setback or was frustrated in some way by a lack of success. Describe the person's thoughts and feelings in as much detail as you can.

2. Make up your own all-star team using the 100 players in this book. Choose a player for each position, including one right-handed and one left-handed pitcher. Pick the players you believe were the greatest in their positions, and then be prepared to defend your choices with some statistics or other evidence of the "greatness" of your selections. When you are done, exchange your list with a friend and compare your choices. After you compare them, reread the entries of all the players about whom you disagree, and then debate whether your players or your friend's players were worthy of being chosen.

INDEX

OUT NOW: